D0777276

MANAGERIALISM FOR ECONOMIC
DEVELOPMENT

STUDIES
IN SOCIAL LIFE

EDITOR:

GUNTHER BEYER

MANAGERIALISM FOR ECONOMIC DEVELOPMENT

Essays on India

S. BENJAMIN PRASAD, Ph. D.
Associate Professor Ohio University

and

ANANT R. NEGANDHI, Ph. D.
Associate Professor Kent State University

MARTINUS NIJHOFF / THE HAGUE / 1968

PRINTED IN THE NETHERLANDS

Economic Development is not the main objective of life on this planet . . . But as a means it is not to be underrated . . . If we want economic development for this purpose . . . we should want also to develop the effectiveness and quality of management . . . But you could have management without development, but you cannot have development without management.

Lord Lionel C. Robbins

FOREWORD

That a developing economy needs management even more than resources is now becoming abundantly clear to all students of growth. There was perhaps a facile assumption in the earlier years that the rate of growth in a developing country depended in almost direct proportion to two factors: the resources available within the country, the land, water, minerals, savings and other relevant inputs; and the initial importation of aid from without, in terms of capital and skills not available within – but the factor of good management was somehow ignored, as also the attitudes of the people and their leadership to growth. These two factors are now coming into their own as being crucial to development and there is a new appreciation of the need for a good supply of well trained managers and providing them with an environment that is permissive and encouraging.

These essays are a timely analysis of this new-felt need, and a valuable source of new leads and hypotheses, for they examine the multi-facets of the problem of India's growth, but with keeping the professional manager squarely in the middle of the study. And after all it is he upon whom the major responsibility for development and growth will depend, given the chance.

The contributors to this symposium are seven young Indians, all management educators of distinction at universities in the United States, and one hopes that they will themselves pick up some of the leads and pursue them.

P. L. Tandon,   Visiting Regents' Lecturer,
Chairman, Hindustan Lever Ltd.,   Graduate School of Business
Bombay, India   Administration,
                                       University of California
                                       Los Angeles, California

TABLE OF CONTENTS

LIST OF TABLES

ABOUT THE CONTRIBUTORS

SAGAR C. JAIN, Ph. D. from Cornell University, is an Assistant Professor at the Graduate School of Business, University of North Carolina, Chapel Hill, North Carolina.

ASHOK KAPOOR, Ph. D. from the University of North Carolina, is an Assistant Professor at the Graduate School of Business, New York University.

S. KANNAPPAN, Ph. D. from Tufts University, is an Associate Professor of Economics at Michigan State University. He is the author of *Business Performance Abroad: The Case Study of Aluminium Limited in India* (1962), and the co-author of *Industrial Relations in India* (1966).

ANANT R. NEGANDHI, Ph. D. from Michigan State University, is on the faculty of the Kent State University. He is the author of *Private Foreign Investment Climate in India* (1966), and the co-author of *The United States Overseas Executive* (1967).

SOM PRAKASH, Ph. D. from the University of Virginia, is an Associate Professor of Economics at Duquesne University, Pittsburgh.

S. BENJAMIN PRASAD, Ph. D. from the University of Wisconsin, is an Associate Professor at Ohio University. He is the editor of *Management in International Perspective* (1967), and *Modern Industrial Management* (1967).

DARAB UNWALLA, Ph. D. from the University of Bombay, is an Associate Professor at the Graduate School of Business Administration, Michigan State University. He is the author of *Textile Technocracy*, and co-author of *The Enterprising Man* (1964).

C. N. VAKIL is Professor Emeritus, University of Bombay, and the noted Indian economist. He has authored several books.

PREFACE

The new countries of Asia and Africa are now concerned, as were the countries of Western Europe in the late eighteenth and early nineteenth centuries, with understanding the process on which economic and social progress of their peoples depends. In the years since World War II, in almost all parts of the literate world, there has been an exceedingly active discussion of "economic development". This is especially true of the United States – books, articles, symposiums, courses, and research projects in the general area of "economic development" attest to this observation. As John K. Galbraith noted a few years ago, "Americans can be more than a little proud of the intensity of interest in the economics of development in these last years in the United States."

There is a plethora of literature in the area of economic development theories, economic planning and economic programming. It has been duly recognized that the underdeveloped countries need economic development and the State ought to play the role of the entrepreneur wherever there is a need. The underlying premise on the part of many scholars and national policy-makers appears to be that development is feasible and that the countries should not only aspire for but *plan* to achieve sustained economic growth or development. The popular instrument for formulating national economic goals has been the Five-Year plans which chart out the strategies for economic development.

This basic premise is valid. But we also think that there appears to be a great need for effective implementation of the planned projects as much as there is a need for careful economic planning.

The scope of what is generally referred to as economic development is vast. Our initial assumption is that economic development, especially as it takes place through industrial projects, has been thwarted in many developing countries as a result of ineffective implementation, that is, ineffective management of industrial projects. This is a result, we surmise, of the lack of attention hitherto paid to the "managerial" aspects in economic development strategies.

An examination of the various theoretical mainstreams of economic development suggests that many economists either assume that "managers" are efficient and capable of implementing the planned industrial projects or do not give sufficient importance to the "managerial" aspects. We think that in the march toward industrialism in any country such factors as capital, technology, and infrastructure are extremely important. But they are in the nature of passive, though vital, agents, and they become activated by the managerial element.

We also subscribe to the view that the instrument of production is the corporate form of industrial organization, public or private. Wherever any productive task is to be performed, the corporate organization becomes ubiquitous and inescapable. Modern productive activity, whether it takes place in an advanced or an advancing country, requires a complex blending of the skills and talents of people into a mosaic of tasks and functions in an effective manner. To this we refer to as "managerialism."

In spite of the fact that the role of "managerialism" is recognized theoretically in economic development planning and strategy, it has received but a cursory treatment from scholars, planners, and national leaders. Only recently have there been some indications to serious discussions on the nature and importance of "managerialism" as a significant input in economic development strategies.

The main purpose of this volume is to elucidate the role of "managerialism" in economic development, with India as a model. We recognize that there are vast differences in the conditions which govern India and other developing countries. However, we think that there are enough similarities in the organization and management of industrial enterprise in India and other developing countries that we could justifiably use the term "model". The optimal way to elucidate the role and significance of "managerialism" in economic development would have been to develop a comprehensive framework and deal empirically with all of the major issues of "managerialism." This is not something which we, as a small team, could accomplish. We have, on the other hand, dealt only with half a dozen issues which we thought were significant and on which we could write with a sense of competence.

This volume is, of course, an outcome of the initial encouragement provided to us by scholars such as Professors C. N. Vakil of India, Frederick Harbison and others of the United States. It is a product of the cooperation of several Indian and American scholars now on the faculties of American Universities. We are grateful to Professor Ernest Dale of the Wharton School, University of Pennsylvania for his review of the original manuscript and to Mr. L. M. Sardana, a doctoral candidate at UCLA, for his help in preparing the manuscript. We also thank Mrs. Virginia Scheuller for fine typing of the manuscript which she had to do several times.

This book, despite its limitations, will hopefully serve its intended purpose if it provides a useful guide to further researchable areas for scores of graduate students who come for advanced study to the United States – especially from developing countries – and if it encourages empirical probing into the managerial aspects of economic development in the developing countries of Asia, Africa and Latin America.

S.B.P. and A.R.N.

PART ONE

MANAGERIALISM: PAST, PRESENT, FUTURE

CHAPTER I

INTRODUCTION

The problems of industrialization in India are in many ways no different from those which confront other developing countries struggling to accelerate economic growth in Asia, Africa, and Latin America. All of the developing nations are in need of industrialization both for restoring balance to their economy and for augmenting the rate of national productivity. They all need to be modernized, to develop a scientific outlook, and enhance the quantum of managerial skills and organizational abilities. As Eugene R. Black recently expressed it[1]:

We know that to escape the predicament of their poverty and to survive in the modern world, the people of Asia, Africa, and Latin America are going to have to increase their productivity... Nobody knows this better than the leaders in those areas who are desperately trying to provide some escape. Yet the word "productivity" commands little meaning or understanding in the developing parts of the world.

It would appear that for the countries of Asia, Africa, and Latin America taken together, economic development has proceeded in the last two decades at an estimated rate close to four per cent per year. This has meant a doubling in the total income of the underdeveloped areas of the world, which is a significant achievement compared to the long preceding era of relative economic stagnation.

Without being critical one could venture to say that all the theories of economic development are ways of looking systematically at the general economic development process. Whether one finds a theory of economic growth, a theory of economic development, or a theory of economic progress, they all relate to the "economics about development or growth," but do not constitute the "economics *for* development." Although economic planning

---

[1] Eugene R. Black, "Technology Alone is not Enough," *Forum* (General Electric Company), Fall, 1966, p. 14.

for development has received considerable treatment at the hands of economists and econometricians, it appears that less admirable has been the case with the issues of implementation.

Deficiencies in the process of implementation, we suspect, are not merely due to technological deficiencies but also, more importantly, due to managerial deficiencies. The general foci of the essays in this volume are on "managerialism" *for* economic development. That is to say, they are concerned with the aspects of effectively managing industrial enterprises both in the private and the public sector.

What do we mean by "managerialism?" First of all, we mean something more than internal "management" of enterprises. Although the concept management is of Western origin and has varied meanings in literature it could be usefully identified as a process which involves effective deployment of human and material resources for purposes of achieving enterprise goals. Second, the term "managerialism" is used to convey a whole spectrum of those activities which are imperative to augment industrialization in a country. That is to say, "managerialism" envelops not only enterprise management but also those activities which need to be performed to develop a conducive environment in which an enterprise could function effectively. So this broad concept is comprised of manifold questions; however, in this volume only a few issues of significance to industrial development are discussed. They are: (1) Is Indian management becoming professionalized? (2) Are Western theories of management organization relevant to the Indian context? (3) Can the applicability of American know-how be empirically determined? (4) Can industrial psychology be successfully applied? and (5) What is the best approach to solve organization and manpower problems in the public sector? (6) What about the related issues of small entrepreneurs, foreign investment, foreign technicians as well as management education?

These questions by no means exhaust the possible set of questions one may raise. But these are the questions in which the authors were mainly interested and had competence to discuss. Thus we recognize that ours is only a partial attempt to articulate the theme of "managerialism."

A brief historical account of management and managers in

India is provided by Sagar Jain in Chapter II. With the aid of more recent empirical data the question of how professional the Indian managers have become is discussed by him in Chapter III.

The theme of Chapter IV is the relevance of two sets of theories, namely, of goal-setting and decision-making. Selecting the relevant elements of these theories, Benjamin Prasad attempts to develop an approach to utilize these theories to build effective industrial organizations.

Mere adaptation of management *in toto* is neither feasible nor desirable. One has to systematically determine which managerial elements must be adopted, and which elements must be adapted. A research approach to determine the applicability is developed by Anant Negandhi in Chapter V.

The public sector in India, and in many other developing countries for that matter, is assuming gigantic proportions. The public sector enterprises in India have been confronted by serious organization and manpower problems. In Chapter VI, the nature of these problems and plausible ways of resolving them is discussed by Subbiah Kannappan.

It is apparent that in underdeveloped countries such as India the supply of entrepreneurs is limited, in the first place, by economic circumstances, and secondly, by the social structure.

In Chapter VII Darab Unwalla addresses himself to the question of what some of the salient characteristics are of the innovating small entrepreneur in India, as compared to his American counterpart, and assesses the prospects which may be in store for the Indian entrepreneur in terms of his contribution to economic development in India.

In his preface to *Educating Tomorrow's Managers* (CED), Theodore Yntema stated that "the quality of college training or business careers affects not only the probable performance of the economy in the hands of the oncoming generation, but the overall quality of higher education, and indeed, the very health of our society." Yntema's frame of reference was the United States and he was specifically referring to the business majors in the colleges and schools of business in the U.S. The CED report, as well as other studies, was primarily concerned with a fundamental question: Are the collegiate schools of business making the needed contribution to the development of business management so vital to the economic performance of the U.S.

In Chapter VIII, the noted economist C. N. Vakil, discusses the issue of management education in India. Management education is a two-sided coin. One relates to education in management for those who are already in some sense managers; the other refers to formal training in management or education for management in the future. Professor Vakil's concern in this chapter is for the latter.

In the postwar developmental literature, both in the United States and abroad, one generally finds considerable support for the point of view that private capital has a vital role to play in accelerating economic development of the underdeveloped areas of the world. Anant Negandhi's concern in his chapter (IX) is to inquire into the perceptions of the foreign investment decision-makers as they relate to the favorable and the unfavorable factors in the investment climate in India. He focusses on the administrative mechanism and suggests how the mechanism could be so modified as to maximize potential investment from abroad. The methodology which he has employed will also permit one to engage in longitudinal studies of the investors' perceptions.

Foreign investment may take various forms but the one which is now in vogue is the joint venture – a tandem pull by both developed and developing countries. One of the vexing problems in joint ventures or foreign collaborations is the internal opposition to advanced management techniques by the partner. Although it is generally stated that joint ventures help to build a new entrepreneurial and managerial class in the developing world as well as foster the development of a variety of ancillary services and manufacturing enterprises, a continually vexing problem has been that of the absence of a working atmosphere of mutual trust and confidence. This shows up in many ways. Ashok Kapoor, in Chapter X, on the basis of his empirical studies, pinpoints the problem in the role of the foreign collaborator.

The purpose of these essays is not directly to offer practical solutions but to suggest research approaches which might point to the practical solutions. They are in the tradition of the "management process" school of thought, and we think at the present and the immediate future this is an adequate form of reference for research on managerialism in India. If these essays, which are partly impressionistic and partly theoretical, generate the interest of the researchers, scholars, and the policy-makers in developing countries, they would have, in our opinion, accomplished their objectives.

CHAPTER 2

OLD STYLE MANAGEMENT

The Industrial Revolution was brought to India by British capitalists who were attracted by India's industrial potential. However, these people were faced with one major dilemma: they did not want to live and tend personally to their investments in India. In order to surmount this problem, these men invented a unique system of absentee management. They formed and registered their companies in England to do business in India, but the directors of these companies did not assume the direct responsibility for the companies' operation and management. Instead, they contracted out these functions to interested Britishers who were either living in India or were willing to go there. This system of management by proxy came to be known as the "managing agency system."[1]

Although the managing agency system was brought into being to overcome the difficulty created by the distance between the place of origin of an industrial proposition and the place of its actual operation, the system was adopted quite widely even where companies were of Indian origin. In retrospect, many factors seem to have contributed to such a development.

Impressed by the prospects of the companies under their management, managing agents increasingly began to promote new companies to which they became self-appointed managing agents. Many of these companies were registered in India. Faced with a drastic shortage of venture capital, inadequate banking facilities and a lack of experience in industrial management,

---

[1] This is a very simplified treatment of the subject. For details see P. S. Lokanathan, *Industrial Organization in India* (London: George Allen & Unwin, 1935) p. 15-43; Vera Anstey, *The Economic Development in India* (London: Longmans, Green & Co., 1929), pp. 113-115; D. R. Samant and M. A. Mulky, *Organization and Finance of Industries in India* (Bombay: Longmans, Green & Co., 1937), pp. 32-34; and D. H. Buchanan, *The Development of Capitalistic Enterprise in India* (New York: MacMillan Co., 1934) pp. 165-171.

many companies formed on Indian initiative also turned to managing agency firms.[2] Also, the material advantages accruing to a promoter when he appointed himself as the managing agent of the promoted company were found to be so great that numerous Indian businessmen, who had accumulated vast fortunes in trading and other activities, installed themselves as promoters and managing agents. Prompted by such factors, the managing agency system became an almost universal characteristic of industrial management in India. Writing in 1937, Samant and Mulky, two well-known observers of Indian management noted that "the number of joint stock companies managed without managing agents is so small, that they can very well be taken as exception proving the general rule."[3]

For the purposes of this discussion it is important that the nature of the managing agency firm and its relationship to the companies which it managed, be fully comprehended. In this regard it should be re-emphasized that the managing firm—and not the boards of directors of the companies under their management—had the real say in matters of policy or operations. This was possible because of the fact that managing agency contracts were signed for long periods—20 to 30 years and even for perpetuity—and these contracts usually gave total and indisputable discretion to managing agents in all matters pertaining to the functioning of the concerned companies. Once this contract was signed, the managing agency firm saw to it that the control of the managed companies did not go out of their hands. This was done mainly through various kinds of financial practices, stock ownership and voting arrangements. Most of the managing agency firms held a substantial number of stocks of the companies under their management. Further, they kept these companies under their obligation through loans and advances. A proven instrument for control existed in the use of stock with special voting rights. Such stock was issued only to the managing agents.[4] In fact, so

---

[2] This process started with what was probably the first Indian joint stock company. See S. M. Rutnagur, editor, *Bombay Industries: The Cotton Mills* (Bombay: *The Indian Textile Journal*, 1927), p. 9.

[3] Samant and Mulky, *op. cit.*, p. 12.

[4] For further details of these practices, see Lokanathan, *op. cit.*, Appendix I to Chapter I, pp. 41-43; Nabagopal Das, *Industrial Enterprise in India* (Calcutta: Orient Longmans, 1956), pp. 77-78; National Council of Applied Economic Research, *The Managing Agency System: A Review of its Working and Prospects of its Future* (Bombay:

complete was the control of managing agents of companies under their management that in most cases they selected the boards of directors of these companies.

After a careful scrutiny of the manner in which the boards of directors of companies under managing agents were constituted, Andrew Brimmer found that in practically every instance several directors came from agency firms, and often, one of these agencies' directors occupied the position of chairman or managing director. His study concluded that the boards of directors of the companies under the managing agency system were "nothing more than a fiduciary body... the managing agency firm is responsible for practically all decisions made in the companies under its control."[5]

Another feature of the system was that a managing agency firm did not restrict its managerial activities to one or two companies or to any specific type of industry. Many of these firms controlled and managed scores of companies in a wide variety of industries. One study showed that 38 managing agency firms were managing more than 600 companies, some of them as many as 40 to 50 companies in more than 20 industries.[6] In addition, the system of "multiple directorship" was quite common. It was found that approximately 100 persons held as many as 1700 directorships of important companies. Of these 100 individuals, 30 held 860 directorships. The top 10 alone held 400 directorships, with two men each on the boards of 50 companies.[7]

It would appear, then, that in the early stages of Indian industrialization, a small group of managing agents, along with those whom they hired for help, composed practically the total population of industrial managers in India. Any discussion regarding the professional status of Indian management as will be taken up in the next chapter, must, therefore, begin with an evaluation of men in managing agencies: their education and

Asia Publishing House, 1959), pp. 67-82; and Raj K. Nigam, *Managing Agencies in India* (First Round: Basic Facts, Department of Company laws, Ministry of Commerce and Industry, Government of India (New Delhi, 1953).

[5] Andrew F. Brimmer, "The Setting of Entrepreneurship in India," Quarterly Journal of Economics (November, 1955) p. 556.

[6] See M. M. Mehta, *Structure of Indian Industries* (Bombay: Popular Book Depot, 1955), pp. 250-252. Also see R. K. Nigam, *op. cit.*; and S. K. Basu, *The Managing Agency System* (Calcutta: The World Press, 1958), pp. 11-46.

[7] M. M. Mehta, *op. cit.*, pp. 261-267.

training, their orientation and values, their organizations and professional activities and their routes of entry and advancement.

The early managers in India

The literature dealing with the managing agents (as distinct from the managing agency system) and the people they hired to help manage their companies, is very sparse. This is particularly true of the period before the 1920's.[8] On the basis of scattered and limited data, the following picture may be reconstructed:

The people who turned to industrial management were from a trading background. This is probably true of the Indian managing agents more than the British. The pioneering group of British managing agents in India came from those British businessmen and traders who had come to India as member of "...the civil and military service, but who perhaps finding their habits better adapted for commercial pursuits, obtained permission to resign their situations and engage in agency and commercial business."[9] This group was later joined by engineers and technicians who were brought to India in order to install machinery and to teach Indians how to operate it, as well as those who had come to India in connection with the purchase of raw materials, the sale of finished products and shipping.[10] The Indian managing agents came from the trading castes of Hindus, Jains, Zoroastrians (popularly known as "Parsees") and Jews.[11]

They were *acquisitive* people who had taken to their new avocation of a managing agency with the hope of making easy and quick money. Basically, they were traders both in their mentality and their approach. In relentless pursuit of profit they were sometimes willing to exploit every person and institution subject to their influence: the company they managed, the people they employed, the consumers they served, and the producers who supplied them.[12]

[8] For a very useful discussion on source material on this and related subjects, see B. N. Ganguli, editor, *Readings in Indian Economic History* (Bombay: Asia Publishing House, 1964).

[9] (British) *Parliamentary Papers 1831-1832*, X, Part II, App. 3, p. 496. Digest of Evidence before the Lords' Select Committee on Affairs of the East India Company.

[10] D. H. Buchanan, *op. cit.*, pp. 142-143.

[11] Buchanan, *op. cit.*, pp. 144-148. Also see his chapters on specific industries. An additional valuable source S. M. Rutnagur, *op. cit.*.

[12] Literature on this subject is rich. The following provide a good and well docu-

Generally the early managing agencies were "firms" as opposed to joint stock companies or corporations. However, the internal organization of the British firms tended to be somewhat different from that of the Indian firms. A British firm was a partnership of several interested persons who were willing to pool their money and talents for a business venture. Each partner headed a department in the firm and served as director, managing director, or senior officer of one or more of the managed companies. The partners would rotate from one department to another and from one company to another if, and when, it was considered desirable. When a partner died or retired from the business, he was not automatically replaced by his son. Often he would be replaced by a senior officer of the firm.[13]

The structure of an Indian firm was influenced predominantly by the larger social system in which a unit of economic activity was coterminous with the familial organization. Accordingly, in Indian firms the oldest male, so long as he was not incapacitated, was the head of the firm. Other males in the family were automatically members in the firm, but they acted under the direction of the family head. Upon death of any member of the firm, his male issues would automatically replace him under well established customs and laws.

At first, nearly all of the managerial and technical personnel who were hired by the managing agents (British as well as Indian) to direct, supervise and control the operations of their various companies, came from Britain and Europe. Considering the fact that the modern industrial process was not native to India, this wholesale importation of managerial and technical talents is not surprising. However, as early as 1887 the process of Indianization of managerial ranks was in full swing.[14] By 1895 the proportion of European (in colloquial usage, all persons from the Occident are Europeans) personnel in Bombay textile mills had fallen to 42.5 per cent.[15] In 1921, for India as a whole, 34.6 per cent of the

mented summary of this literature: Lokanathan, *op. cit.*, Samant and Mulky, *op. cit.*; S. K. Basu, *op. cit.*, and National Council of Applied Economic Research, *op. cit.*
[13] Wilfred Russell, *Indian Summer* (Bombay, 1951), p. 58.
[14] "The largest mill-owner (of Bombay)is a Parsee millionaire, Sir Dinshaw Manaeckjee Petit; he runs seven mills, all well managed, many of them superintended without the aid of any European foreman." Inspector Meade King in "Annual Report of the Chief Inspector of Factories and Workshops (in Great Britain) for 1887," *Parliamentary Papers*, 1888 Cmd., 5328, p. 116.
[15] Rutnagar, *op. cit.*, p. 294.

managers were Europeans.[16] By 1925 this percentage was 28.4.[17] Thus by the mid 1920's, nearly three out of every four managerial-supervisory positions were held by Indians. The imported talent was usually employed in higher level jobs.[8]

According to one source, in 1925, a little over 50 per cent of Indian managers employed in Bombay mills were Zoroastrians, 17 per cent were Hindus, 3 per cent were Jews and 1.5 per cent were Muslims.[19] It should be pointed out that in Bombay mills the Zoroastrians dominated not only the ranks of the salaried managers, but also the ranks of managing agents and owners.[20]

Very little is known about the education and training of the managers during this period. But because of the fact that there was little or no facility for formal education and training in business or industrial management at that time, either in India or in Britain, or any other country,[21] these people could not have had any systematized education and training in this field. Some of the people must have had their training in engineering and accounting. But a large majority of the managers were "managers" either because they had learned their business through a long apprenticeship rooted in the trial and error method,[22] or because they had inherited their positions.

[16] *Census of India*, 1921, I, Part II, p. 264.

[17] Buchanan, *op. cit.*, p. 211.

[18] Further details are available on selected industries. For coal mining see *Census of India*, 1921, I, pp. 250-251, *Ibid.*, I, Part II, pp. 250 and 302. These data are also available in Buchanan, *op. cit.*, pp. 269-270. For the jute industry, see D. R. Sallace, *Romance of Jute* (London: W. Thacker & Co., 1927).

[19] Rutnagar, *op. cit.*, p. 294.

[20] Buchanan, *op. cit.*, p. 211, footnote 52.

[21] The Wharton School of Finance and Commerce, founded in 1881, was the first Business School not only in the United States, but probably in the world. In India, university level courses in business and industrial administration were not offered until 1953. For details, see Ministry of Scientific Research and Cultural Affairs, Government of India, *Report of a Visit to the United States of America (15th March to 15th May 1959) by the Indian Management Education Study Team* (Delhi: Govt. of India Press, 1959). The commerce education in India is also no more than 60-65 years old. See Syed Nurullah and J. P. Naik, *A History of Education in India* (Bombay, 1943); India (Dominion) University Education Commission, *The Report*, Vol. I (1949); and All-India Council for Technical Education, Ministry of Scientific Research and Cultural Affairs, Government of India, *Report of the Special Committee for Commerce Education* (Delhi, 1961). For an interesting note on Management Education, see Appendix B in this volume.

[22] The following quote is very enlightening in this connection: "A typical (jute) mill has between 15 and 20 European assistants, one to every 200 or 300 Indians (laborers); these are almost invariably Scotsmen, poor boys from the farms and towns about Dundee, who have learned their business in that mother of jute manufacturing." Buchanan, *op. cit.*, p. 246. Also see Wallace, *op. cit.*

The managers had little or no identity of their own apart from that of owners of business, employers, engineers or accountants. Consequently, no need was felt to organize a management association. However, several trade associations as well as mill-owners' associations were in active existence. The Indian Jute Mills Association was organized about 1884, by the British managing firms to cope with a bad case of overproduction.[23] The Bombay Mill Owners Association had come into being even earlier, in 1875.[24] It was followed by the Ahmedabad Mill Owners Association. Both of the associations were in the hands of Indians and were organized to protect the interests of the cotton textile industry. Among the other well known trade associations were the Indian Mining Federation (1892) and The Indian Tea Association (1881). In addition there were several chambers of commerce organized on a regional and ethnic basis.[25]

From the data presented above, it is clear that the managers of early industrial enterprises were grossly lacking in all the attributes of a profession. It is as well that they made no pretense of being "professionals" at that time.

The Old System Changeth

The system of industrial management in India remained basically the same until the 1930's. However, the managing agency system came under increasing fire from various quarters, including labor, stockholders of the managed companies,[26] the academic community, social workers and politicians. Among the major charges levelled against the system were (1) that managing agents held on to the companies in perpetuity by both fair and foul means; (2) that they manipulated the company stocks for personal gains; (3) that they used all kinds of devices and procedures to fatten their own remunerations for "managing" the companies;

[23] W. L. Cotton, *Handbook of Commercial Information for India*, second edition (Calcutta, 1924).

[24] See S. D. Sakletwala, *History of the Millowners Association, Bombay, 1875-1930* (Bombay: The Millowners Association, 1931).

[25] For details see Cotton, *op. cit.*

[26] In Bombay, the stockholders of the managed companies organized themselves into a body, known as Bombay Shareholders Association, to safeguard their interests. For a sample of their grievances and activities, see their *Memorandum on Managing Agents* (Bombay, 1949).

and (4) that they used the funds of companies for their own business purposes and made the companies bear the brunt if there were losses.

In 1936 these criticisms culminated in several amendments to the Indian Companies Act of 1913. These amendments sought to correct some of the more glaring malpractices in the system. But these changes did not prove to be adequate. Therefore, the Act was again amended in 1951 by putting new restrictions on the managing agents. Even these measures did not satisfy the critics of the system. Finally, with the passage of the Indian Companies Act, 1956 the Government of India assumed the power to prohibit managing agencies in any industry or business. This new power has put the system under effective probation. This law has placed many new limitations on the tenure, transfer and vacation of office, conditions of office, remuneration, and activities of the managing agents. These provisions may be summarized as follows:

1. All appointments and reappointments of managing agents to a company are subject to government approval which will be accorded if (a) such an appointment is not found to be against public interest; (b) the proposed managing agent is a "fit and proper" person for the office; and (c) the conditions of the agreement are fair and reasonable.

2. The maximum term of office of a managing agent for initial appointment is set at fifteen years, and to ten years for re-appointments. All those holding office at the time of the passage of the Act were required to seek reappointment by August 15, 1960.

3. Inclusion of any provision for succession to office by inheritance or devise in managing agency agreements is prohibited. Now an heir or devisee of the managing agent is allowed to hold office only if the government is satisfied that he is a fit and proper person.

4. A managing agency is not allowed to manage more than ten companies. Further no person is allowed to hold office as director in more than twenty companies and as managing director in more than two companies.

5. The managing agent of a company is to exercise his power subject to the supervision, control and direction of the Board of Directors. The matters on which the managing agent may

act only after the previous consent of the Board of Directors are also specified. These include the appointment of managers and other staff of the companies and the purchase and sale of capital assets at prices outside the limits prescribed by the Board.

6. A managing agent may appoint only two directors where the strength of the Board exceeds five and one where it does not exceed five.

7. A ceiling has been put on the remuneration of the managing agents. It is not to exceed 11 per cent of the net profits of the managed company, with a minimum of Rs 40,000 (approximately $ 5,333).

8. A managing agent is required to limit his activities only to those prospects which are necessary for efficient management. More specifically, an agent and his associates are prohibited to act as sales and purchase agents of the managed company for extra remuneration; he cannot use the funds of one company for another at will; he cannot make investment on behalf of the company at will; and he cannot engage on his own account in any business directly competing with that of a company managed by him.

Increasing governmental surveillance and control of managing agencies have, indeed, played a crucial part in modifying the role, structure and functions of the managing agency system. But other developments have also been significant. For one thing, the public sector has been expanding rapidly. Prior to 1947, the government had virtually no industrial and business enterprise in the country. According to a Government of India report, in 1961 the total investment (paid-up capital) in government-owned companies was Rs 4,772 millions.[27] These figures did not include those governmental enterprises which were owned and operated directly by various departments of the Indian Government (for example, railways; post, telegraph, and telephone; All India Radio) or were statutory corporations (for example, Air India International, Indian Airlines Corporation, Life Insurance Corporation) which are not "companies" under the Indian Companies Act. Obviously if these enterprises were also to be

[27] Research and Statistics Division, Company Law Administration, Government of India, *Information Broad Sheet*, no. 2 (1961).

taken into account, the investment in the public sector would be considerably more than shown by the above figure.

Secondly, the foreign investments in India have been also rising steadily. In 1959, the Reserve Bank of India estimated that the total foreign investment in the private sector to be Rs. 6,107 millions,[28] which was nearly one third of the total corporate investment in India.[29] Two-thirds of this foreign capital is British,[30] invested primarily in companies managed by scores of British managing the following agencies. The significant thing about the foreign capital is that the relative share of non-British capital (American, Canadian, West German and from other countries) has been rising,[31] and most of this capital has been invested in companies which are outside the managing agency system.

Both public sector enterprises and new foreign companies have rejected managing through Boards of Directors. Since these two groups of companies form a large proportion of the corporate sector of the Indian economy, and since the system of direct management adopted by them has proved to be at least as efficient as the managing agency system, there is a growing realization that a company can do without a managing agent. This realization has encouraged many companies in the private sector to seek no aid from managing agents in either their organization or their management.[32] Further, several companies which were previously managed by the managing agents, have decided to go on their own.[33] *These developments have greatly reduced the importance of the managing agency system in India's corporate sector.* According to a relatively recent study, in 1954-55 there were 3,944 managing agencies in India managing 5,055 joint stock companies, or, 17.1 per cent of the total number of joint stock companies in India. Further, this study found that

[28] *Reserve Bank of India Bulletin,* May 1961, p. 674.

[29] See the statement by B. R. Bhagat, Deputy Minister of Finance, Government of India in the Lok Sabha on April 13, 1961 as reported in *Indian News* (Washington, D. C., May 1, 1961).

[30] *Reserve Bank of India Bulletin,* May 1961, p. 685.

[31] *Ibid.*, p. 685. Also see Anant R. Negandhi, *Private Foreign Investment Climate in India* (East Lansing: Division of Research, Michigan State University, 1965).

[32] Of the 1448 companies formed during 1955-56, only 29 were to be managed by managing agents. For details, see S. K. Basu, *op. cit.*, pp. 188-207.

[33] See G. L. Mehta, "Managerial Revolution in India," *Indian Management*, December 1962, pp. 12-15.

the companies managed by managing agents had paid-up capital totalling Rs. 4,654 millions, which was 48 per cent of the aggregate paid-up capital of the entire corporate sector.[34]

In increasing recognition of the legislative pressure and the success of the direct management model, the managing agencies themselves are undergoing two main changes. First, they are rejecting the "family firm" structure in favor of the joint stock form.[35] By doing so, they are willing to subject themselves to greater legal and public scrutiny than they would have undergone as a family firm. Also by throwing open their share capital to the public, they are demonstrating their willingness to share their gains. It may be argued that this is a price which they must pay to survive in the face of hostile public and political opinion. There may even be some tax (or other) economic advantages in making such a change. Regardless of the motives for reorganization of the structure of managing agencies, the fact remains that this change is taking place and that it permits a closer public scrutiny in the affairs of these businesses than was otherwise possible. Further, this revision of the managing agencies is changing the status of the managing agents from owners of their firm to stockholders' representatives and managers. This, in turn makes the managing agents accountable to their stockholders for their efficiency, integrity, creativity and productivity.

The second major change is in the hiring policies of the managing agents. Managing agencies have been widely noted and often criticized for blatant nepotism and favoritism in their personnel practices.[36] However, under growing pressure for superior performance, these agencies have started placing emphasis upon the knowledge, training and skills of a person rather

[34] Nigam, *op. cit.*

[35] According to R. K. Nigam, *op. cit.*, in 1954-55, 1422 out of 3944 managing agencies were joint stock companies. Although such agencies accounted for only 36 per cent of the total, they managed 45 per cent of all the companies under managing agents. Further, the paid-up capital of the companies managed by agency houses organized on joint stock company basis was 80 per cent of the total for the companies under the agency system.

[36] See S. D. Mehta, *The Indian Cotton Textile Industry: An Economic Analysis* (Bombay: Textile Association, 1953), p. 84; S. P. Acharya, *Business Organization, Administration and Management in India Today* (Bombay: Taraporavela Sons & Co., 1952) Second ed. pp. 97-98; Charles A. Myers, "Management in India": in Harbison and Myers, *op. cit.*, p. 141; and Leo R. Werts, *Observations and Suggestions Concerning India's Manpower Program*, Directorate of Manpower, Ministry of Home Affairs, Government of India (New Delhi, 1960), mimeographed, p. 89.

than his social origin. This tendency to bureaucratize (using the term in Weberian sense) has received support from an additional source. Until recently, most industrial enterprises in India were concerned with production of commodities which were based on relatively simple techniques (e.g., textiles, sugar, cement, paper, etc.). But, as the country has increasingly turned toward producing capital goods, machine tools, chemical products and the like, manufacturing techniques have become more complex. To operate and manage these new and complex industries, highly trained engineers, scientists and managers have become necessary. In order to find sufficient people of such talent, employers must now look far and wide, beyond their families, castes, religions and geographical regions.

CHAPTER 3

THE NEW BREED OF MANAGERS

"Is the Indian manager becoming professionalized?" This is the question with which this chapter is concerned. Historical data were analyzed in the previous chapter to discuss this question of paramount importance in India's economic development.

Attracted by high prestige and other rewards enjoyed by the people in professions, an increasing number of occupations are endeavoring to gain such recognition.[1] To this end they make all kinds of efforts ranging from acquiring many of the trappings of the established professions to initiating deep rooted changes in their education and training, behavior and practice, aspirations and relationships. However, what makes an occupation a profession is largely a moot question both from a theoretical and a methodological viewpoint.[2] Although the debate over the boundary between a "profession" and a "non-profession" continues, two broad conclusions seem to emerge. First, professional and non-professional behavior should not be viewed as a dichotomous relationship but as relative points on a continuum. To quote Bernard Barber's succinct statement on this subject:

There is no absolute difference between professional and other kinds of occupational behavior, but only relative differences with respect to certain attributes common to all occupational behavior. Some occupational behavior, seen in the light of these attributes,...is fully professional; other behavior is

[1] Nelson Foote, in his "The Professionalization of Labor in Detroit" *American Journal of Sociology*, Vol. 58 (1953) pp. 371-380, has argued that these efforts have reached their logical conclusion which is demonstrated by the fact that "labor itself is becoming professionalized."

[2] A good illustration of this debate is to be found in comparing Bernard Barber, "Some Problems in the Sociology of the Professions," *Daedalus, Journal of the American Academy of Arts and Sciences*, Vol. 92 (Fall 1963), pp. 667-683; and Earnest Greenwood, "Attributes of a Profession," *Social Work*, Vol. 2 (July 1957). Both Barber and Greenwood have made extensive surveys of literature on professions. Their conclusions on their findings are substantially different. This difference highlights the point regarding lack of agreement on the concept of a profession.

partly professional, and some can be thought of as barely or not at all professional... Professionalism is a matter of degree.[3]

Second, the following attributes figure prominently in discussions pertaining to "a model of profession"[4]:

1. A high degree of generalized and systematic knowledge which serves as a base for the professional's decisions and actions in concrete situations. This knowledge is often a mixture of theory and skills, and is gained through extensive education and training. Because of such training, a professional is expected to know more than others in his professed field of competence.

2. A professional *culture* characterized by a formal professional association, a code of ethics, values, norms and symbols.

3. Community interests are given precedence over individualized self-interest. Indeed, self-interest is not altogether sacrificed for the sake of larger interests of the community but "is subserved indirectly."

It is generally realized that the model of profession will be much sharper and clearer than the actuality that confronts us when we "observe the occupational scene"[5] and that "few, if any, professions conform fully to the criteria attributes."[6]

Discussing the various types of management, Harbison and Myers[7] have argued that a "professional management" is the highest form of management. They have defined professional management as that kind of enterprise management in which major policy-making positions and nearly all other positions in the hierarchy are held by persons on the bases of alleged or

[3] Bernard Barber, *op. cit.*, pp. 671-72.

[4] In addition to the writings of Barber and Greenwood cited above, see Talcot Parsons, "The Professions and Social Structure," *Social Forces*, Vol. 17 (1939) pp. 457-467; W. J. Goode, "Community Within a Community: The Professions," *American Sociological Review*, Vol. 22 (1957) pp. 194-200; R. K. Merton, "Some Thoughts on Professions in American Society," *Brown University Papers* No. 27, 1960; E. C. Hughes, "Professions," *Daedalus*, 92 (Fall 1962) pp. 655-668; A. M. Carr-Saunders and P. A. Wilson, "Professions" *Encyclopedia of Social Sciences* (1934), pp. 476-480; Abraham Flexner, "Is Social Work a Profession?" *Proceedings of the National Conference of Charities* and Collection (1915); Kenneth S. Lynn, editor, *Professions in America* (New York: Houghton Mifflin, 1965); Louis D. Brandeis, *Business: A Profession* (Boston: Hale, Cushman and Flint, 1933).

[5] Greenwood, *op. cit.*

[6] John C. Kidneigh, "Social Work as a Profession," *Social Work Year Book* (1960), p. 570.

[7] Frederick Harbison and Charles A. Myers, *Management in the Industrial World* (New York: McGraw-Hill, 1959), pp. 76-77.

demonstrated technical competence rather than on relationships to a family or to a political regime." Sociologists will immediately recognize the Weberian model of bureaucracy[8] in these observations.

This brief discussion of the attributes of a profession serves as a necessary background for a systematic examination of the process of professionalization of the Indian managers. Here the concern is not with the question as to whether "management" or "business" *per se* is a "profession."[9] Rather it is with the Indian manager and his growing claim to professional status.

The new system of management in India is producing a new kind of manager whose education and training is continuously rising, and[4]who is growing conscious of his image as a "manager." The new Indian manager shows an increasing tendency to begin his job history with a managerial or an equivalent position, and generally, is hired for his merit. The following data presented to support these conclusions were collected in 1963 from a sample of 1982 middle and top level managers (Indian nationals only) from manufacturing and processing concerns from all over India. Only those enterprises which employed a minimum of 2,000 persons were included. These enterprises were drawn from all the three sectors of the economy: public, foreign, and Indian private.[10]

The data are divided into four groups according to the length of the service of the managers: 10 years or less, 11 to 20 years,

---

[8] See H. H. Gerth and C. W. Mills, Translators and editors, *From Max Weber* (New York: Oxford University Press, 1958), chapter on "Bureaucracy."

[9] Those interested in this question will gain a great deal from Brandeis, *op. cit.,* Bernard Barber, "Is American Business Becoming Professionalized? Analysis of a Social Ideology," In E. A. Tiryakian (ed.) *Sociological Theory, Values and Sociocultural Change: Essays in Honor of Piterim A. Sorokin* (New York: The Free Press of Glencoe, 1963), pp. 121-145; R. H. Tawney, *The Acquisitive Society* (New York: Harvest Books, 1920), Chapter 7, "Industry as a Profession;" Ralph J. Cordiner, *New Frontiers for Professional Managers* (New York: McGraw-Hill, 1956), Wallace B. Donham, "The Emerging Profession of Business," *Harvard Business Review* (1927) 406-19; W. D. Patterson, "Business: Our Newest Profession," *The Saturday Review*, January 19, 1957; The Editors of *Fortune*, with the collaboration of Russell W. Davenport, *U.S.A.: The Permanent Revolution* (Englewood Cliffs, N.J.: Prentice-Hall, 1951); and Frank W. Abrams, "Management's Responsibilities in a Complex World," *Harvard Business Review*, 29, (1951).

[10] For a detailed account of the sample as well as methods and techniques of this study, see Sagar C. Jain, *Social Origins and Careers of Industrial Managers in India.* Unpublished doctoral dissertation, Cornell University, 1964, pp. 211-248. The data on the changing character of Indian managers which are reported in the present paper are not available in this doctoral thesis.

21 to 30 years and 31 years or more. Since the data for this study were collected in 1963, the first group (10 years or less) includes those managers who took their first job between 1953 and 1963. Similarly, the managers in the second groups started their careers between 1943-1953; the third group between 1933-43; and the fourth group between 1923-33, or even earlier. Henceforth in this discussion they will be referred to as generations 4, 3, 2, and 1 respectively.

These four generations are compared for a number of factors, including education, career-path, occupational origin, religion, caste and native state, in order to bring out the change in their character. In this connection the following facts are presented.

EDUCATION

Emphasis on formal education has increased.

A comparison of the formal education among the four generations of managers showed that the successive generations had increasingly higher education. Nearly sixty per cent of those who had started their careers 31 years ago or earlier were not college graduates, and ten per cent had not even finished high school. The proportions of such managers have declined steadily, and they account for only eleven per cent and zero per cent respectively among the youngest group. (See Table 1.)

TABLE 1

Education among four generations of the Indian managers

	Generation 4 (N = 377)	Generation 3 (N = 742)	Generation 2 (N = 678)	Generation 1 (N = 183)
Less than High School	0%	0%	2%	10%
High School	1	2	9	16
Some College	4	4	7	12
Technical diploma	6	12	19	21
Bachelor's degree	20	23	19	14
Master's degree or more	69	59	44	27
Total	100%	100%	100%	100%

Source of data: 1963 Study, *op. cit.*

Here it may be of interest to note that a 1959 Fortune magazine study found that 67 per cent of U.S. executives were college graduates.[11] Two studies of British managers made in the mid-fifties found that only 19 per cent to 26 per cent had college degrees, and that as many as 20 per cent to 25 per cent had less than a high school education.[12] These figures show that the Indian manager compares favorably with the managers of the world's most industrialized countries in terms of his educational background.

Formal education and training in management is increasing

When these four generations of managers were compared for their formal training in management, three facts emerged:

The proportion of those who have joined business enterprises with a graduate level education in management has risen steadily from one per cent in the first generation to four per cent in the second generation, to seven per cent in the third generation, to fourteen per cent in the fourth generation.

The proportion of those who came to occupy their managerial positions after going through a formal "management-traineeship," has been increasing: 12% to 21% to 26% to 33% respectively.

Lastly, more younger managers are attending short-term courses in management, organized by various education, governmental and professional bodies. The proportion of managers who had attended at least one such course in India (or some other country) has increased from 21 per cent in the first generation group to 32 per cent in the second generation group, to 36 per cent in the third generation group. The figure for the youngest group declined to 25 per cent. This dip in the curve probably has been caused by the reluctance of the companies to invest in the training of those who are still relatively "green."

CAREER PATHS

During the last forty years, there have been two significant changes in the career patterns of the Indian managers. First,

[11] "1700 Top Executives," *Fortune* (November, 1959).
[12] The Acton Society Trust, *Management Succession* (London: The Acton Society Trust, 1956); and R. V. Clements, *Managers* (London: George Allen and Unwin).

they tend to begin their career at an older age. Those who went to work more than 30 years ago, did so at an average age of 20.9 years. The following two generations had averages ages of 22.7 years and 22.6 years respectively at the time of their first job. Those in the youngest generation did not go to work until they were 23.3 years old on the average. This tendency to begin careers at a later age seems to be mainly a consequence of the fact that the younger generation of Indian managers have been spending more time getting a formal education. While the oldest group of managers spent an average of 12.7 years as students, the figures for the following three successive groups are 14.0 years, 15.1 years and 15.4 years.

The second change is in relation to the kinds of jobs with which they started their careers. More of the first generation's managers had begun their careers as laborers (19%) than as managers – management trainees and executives (16%). In the youngest generation, while nobody came up from the ranks of laborers, 49 per cent were hired directly into managerial positions. Similar changes are noted in relation to white collar (clerical and retail sale) jobs and the professions (doctors, lawyers, engineers, professors, scientists, accountants and auditors): while the former category has shrunk from 29 per cent in the first generation to 7

TABLE 2

Career paths of four generations of the Indian managers

First Occupational Job Held	4th Generation (N = 368)	3rd Generation (N = 716)	2nd Generation (N = 646)	1st Generation (N = 170)
Laborer	0%	2%	8%	19%
White-collar worker	7	17	23	29
Foreman-supervisor	21	25	22	21
Management trainee	33	26	21	12
Business executive (minor)	16	7	5	3
Business executive (major)	0	1	1	1
Business owner	1	1	1	1
Professional person	22	19	14	10
Government officer	0	1	2	3
Military officer	0	1	3	1
All Occupations	100%	100%	100%	100%

Source of data: 1963 Study, *op. cit.*

per cent in the fourth, the latter category has grown from 10 per cent to 22 per cent. Table 2 presents further details on this subject. In all, these data point out that in earlier days, a man became a manager by gradually rising from low level jobs. To-day, young people with a high level of education and training are making direct entry into managerial positions.

OCCUPATIONS BACKGROUND

The younger generations of managers not only show a greater tendency to start their careers with managerial jobs, they also show a greater tendency to come from families of managers, administrators and professional men. (See Table 3.) When we compare the youngest generation of managers with the oldest generation, we find that, on the one hand, the proportion of the sons of business executives, government officials and professional men has risen from 37 per cent to 60 per cent, and, on the other hand, that the proportion of those whose fathers were laborers, small farmers and clerical workers has fallen from 44 per cent to 20 per cent.

RELIGION

Table 4 presents data on the religions of the four generations of managers and the Indian male population. From this table it may be noted that the religious distribution of managers has steadily moved closer to that of the Indian male population through successive generations. This in turn may suggest that in earlier days there was considerable religious discrimination in the hiring of managers, and that such discrimination is now de-clining. On the basis of these data such a conclusion would be hasty, for it may be pointed out that a group's ability to produce managers depends not only on the opportunities afforded to it for entry into management but also on the merit (education, training, etc.,) of its members as well as their interest in business careers. As a matter of fact, the observed disparities between the religious distribution of the Indian male population and earlier

TABLE 3

Occupation of fathers of four generations of the Indian managers

Occupation	Generation 4 (N = 370)	Generation 3 (N = 729)	Generation 2 (N = 660)	Generation 1 (N = 171)
Laborer	0%	1%	1%	3%
Small farm operator	7	6	8	16
Large farm owner	3	5	6	3
White-collar worker	14	16	21	25
Government official	20	21	17	13
Business executive	16	12	12	11
Professional man	24	21	22	13
Business owner	17	18	13	16
	100%	100%	100%	100%

TABLE 4

Religions of four generations of the Indian managers and Indian male populations

Religion	Generation 4 (N = 377)	Generation 3 (N = 742)	Generation 2 (N = 678)	Generation 1 (N = 183)	Indian Male Population*
Hindu	85%	83%	80%	78%	84.91%
Muslim	1	1	1	1	9.96
Christian	3	4	4	4	2.23
Sikh	2	1	2	3	1.88
Jain	5	6	4	3	0.46
Zoroastrian	2	4	8	10	0.03
Other religions	2	2	1	1	0.53
	100	100	100	100	100.00

* Computed from Census of India, Paper No. 2 of 1953, "Religion – 1951 Census" (Delhi, 1953).

generations of managers, are not so much a function of religious discrimination as it is a function of uneven distribution of education and business interests among these various religions. As years have passed, the spread of education has become more even. This in turn has reduced the initial religious disparities among the managers. Further, the influence of religion on the career choice seems to have been declining. This in turn must contribute toward increasing balance between religious distribution of the population and the managers. However, the question of discrimination cannot be entirely ruled out. Increasing representation of Hindus and Jains in the successive generations of the managers correlates too well with the growth of Hindu and Jain enterprises to not cast any suspicion on this account. When religions of the employers were cross tabulated with the

TABLE 5

Religions of the Managers and the owners of various groups of concerns in the Indian private sector

(Figures in parentheses indicate degrees of representation enjoyed by the religions in relation to their shares in the male population of India, 1951. Proportionate representation = 1.)

Religion of manager	Religion of Owners				
	Hindu	*Jain*	*Zoroastrian*	*Hindu & Sikh*	*Mixed**
Jain	7.0	15.2	0.4	0.0	3.1
	(15.22)	(33.04)	(0.87)	(6.74)	(0.00)
Zoroastrian	1.9	1.1	27.2	3.1	0.0
	(63.33)	(36.67)	(906.66)	(103.33)	(0.00)
Sikh	0.5	1.5	1.7	18.8	0.0
	(0.27)	(0.80)	(0.90)	(10.0)	(0.00)
Muslims	0.2	1.5	1.3	0.0	26.7
	(0.02)	(0.15)	(0.13)	(0.00)	(2.68)
Christian	0.5	1.1	2.9	0.0	13.3
	(0.22)	(0.49)	(1.30)	(0.00)	(5.96)
Buddhist and Jew	0.0	0.0	0.4	0.0	0.0
	(0.22)	(0.49)	(1.30)	(0.00)	(5.96)
	(0.00)	(0.00)	(6.67)	(0.00)	(0.00)
All Religions	100.0%	100.0%	100.0%	100.0%	100.0%
100% =	425	276	239	32	15

* Control of the concern is shared more or less equally by Hindus, Muslims, and foreigners.

religions of the managers (Table 5) it was found that there was a definite tendency on the part of the employers to favor people from their respective religions. However, the religious consideration did not blind them to job merits. This is seen from two sets of facts:

First, Table 5 shows that the Zoroastrians, who rank number one for education and rank very high for business and business-related professional interest, have a greater representation in Hindu enterprises than Hindus themselves, a greater representation in the Hindu-Sikh enterprises than Hindus and Sikhs. Similarly the Jains, who have more education than Hindus and Sikhs and who rank first for business orientation, have a greater representation in Hindu and Hindu-Sikh enterprises than Hindus. Further, in enterprises in which Muslims enjoy substantial ownership and control, they (Muslims) have less representation than Christians who are their superiors in education.

Secondly, when the education of the managers from a favored religion was compared with that of managers from other religions no significant differences were found. The above discussion leads us to conclude that although employers have shown an increasing tendency to hire their managers from their own religion, the primary basis of hiring has been "merit." Religion seems to be taken into consideration only after a candidate is found acceptable on the basis of his education and training.

CASTE

Table 6 provides a picture of how the caste-distribution of the managers has been changing over the years. In the first generation, the Brahmins accounted for 47 per cent and the farmer-warriors for 16 per cent. A steady decline through the next three generations have brought their shares to 37 per cent and 11 per cent respectively in the fourth generation. Their loss has been the gain of the trading castes which have increased their share from 16 per cent in the first generation to 30 per cent in the fourth.

With a majority of the private Indian enterprises under the control of the member of the trading castes, the growing strength of the members of these castes among managers suggests a growing tendency toward casteism in Indian industry. But, in fact, the situation in relation to caste is very similar to the above noted situation in relation to religion. The relative importance of a caste among managers has been largely a function of its educational rank. Trading castes are latecomers in the field of higher and professional education. But once they realized the importance of such education, they have gone after it with zeal. Since higher education is expensive, the trading castes due to their superior economic ability have been in a better position to afford it. This, in turn, has made the trading caste an increasingly important source of supply of managerial talent. Further, in view of their traditional business orientation, an educated person from a trading caste is more inclined to seek a career in business than those whose traditional orientation has been toward farming, priestly and scholarly occupations, civil or military service.

Parenthetically, it should be noted that employers do show an increasing tendency to favor people of their own caste. How-

TABLE 6

Castes of four generations of the Indian managers

(Data include only the Hindu managers)

Caste	Generation 4 (N = 312)	Generation 3 (N = 507)	Generation 2 (N = 529)	Generation 1 (N = 136)
Brahmins	37%	39%	45%	47%
Trading Castes	30	22	18	16
Professional Castes	21	23	22	19
Farming and Warrior Castes	11	15	14	16
Other Interior Castes		1	1	1
Low Service Castes	1	0	0	1
	100	100	100	100

Note: The four great divisions of Hindu Society into *Brahman, Ksatriya, Vaisya* and *Sudra*, are probably historically the earliest classifications. For an interesting discussion of castes and their influence on economic development in India see Robert O. Tilman, "The Influence of Caste on Economic Development" in Ralph Braibanti and Joseph J. Spengler (eds.), *Administration and Economic Development in India* (Durham: Duke University Press, 1963) P. 202-223.

ever, caste, like religion, is given only a secondary importance in a hiring decision. To be hired, a candidate must have the required "technical" qualifications for the job.

REGIONAL ORIGIN

In earlier years Gujarat and Maharastra occupied dominant positions as sources of supply of managers. Together they contributed 33 per cent of the managers in the first generation. But the importance of these two states as a source of managerial manpower has been steadily declining, so much so that their total share in the fourth generation comes to no more than 19 per cent. The opposite is true of West Bengal, Rajasthan and Punjab. West Bengal's contribution rose from 19 per cent in the first generation to 28 per cent in the fourth, Rajasthan's from one per cent to 5 per cent, and Punjab's from 11 per cent to 17 per cent respectively. All other states have more or less maintained status quo (See Table 7.)

Several factors seem to have caused the shift from Gujarat-Maharastra to West Bengal, Rajasthan and Punjab. Probably the most important factor has been the change in the focus of industrial enterprise in India. It was pointed out earlier that the production of capital goods, iron and steel and chemicals had gained increasing importance. During the last fifteen years the government has sought to develop such industries. However, the engineers and managers necessary to man these large and complex enterprises have been in short supply. The Indian Planning Commission estimated that during the Second Five Year Plan period while 85,000 engineers were needed, only 58,000 could be made available. According to the Commission the shortage would continue through the Third Five Year Plan.[13] As a result of these shortages the managerial labor market has been steadily acquiring a national scope. This in turn is forcing a more perfect balance between the manager-productivity of a region and its educational development than had existed previously. Here it should be pointed out that Bengal, Punjab and Gujarat rank 1,

[13] Government of India, Planning Commission, *Third Five Year Plan* (Delhi, 1961), p. 172.

2 and 3 for educational development. The rank order of these states for manager-productivity for the first generation is 2, 3 and 1 respectively. But in the fourth generation, their rank order has changed 1, 2 and 3 just as it is for education.

Several other factors have also contributed to the changes in the manager-productivity of the states. Since 1947, the foreign companies have been under considerable governmental pressure to Indianize their managerial ranks. As a result, these companies have been hiring increasing numbers of Indian Nationals for managerial positions. Since most of these companies operate out of Calcutta, they have tended to hire more people from West Bengal than any other state.

Emergence of Marwarees – the trading caste Hindus and Jains from Rajasthan – in recent years as a dominant group of industrial employers must also influence the status of the states with regard to manager-productivity. Although Marwaree enterprises are scattered all over India, Calcutta is considered to be their main base. As a result of their location, they, like the foreign companies, have hired a sizeable proportion of the managers from West Bengal. In addition they have attracted many people from their home state (Rajasthan) and a neighboring state of Punjab.

TABLE 7

Regional origins of four generations of the Indian managers

State	Generation 4 (N = 377)	Generation 3 (N = 742)	Generation 2 (N = 678)	Generation 1 (N = 183)
Andhra	1%	3%	3%	4%
Bihar	2	2	2	3
Gujarat	13	16	16	22
Kerala	4	8	6	7
Madhya Pradesh	1	0	1	2
Madras	7	7	8	8
Maharastra	6	10	12	11
Mysore	6	8	9	4
Orissa	2	1	1	0
Punjab	17	11	11	11
Rajasthan	5	3	2	1
Uttar Pradesh	8	7	6	8
West Bengal	28	24	23	19
All States	100%	100%	100%	100%

Uneven rates of industrial growth of the states seem to be yet another contributory factor. Those which have been going through a rapid industrial expansion are likely to be under greater pressure to produce managers than those whose rate of industrial growth has been slow.

To conclude the discussion on the regional origins of the managers, it should be stated that the most significant change which has taken place on this account over the years is that the managerial labor market is taking a national dimension. This has been happening primarily because of a shortage of managerial talent.[14] As a result of systematic and effective manpower planning much of this shortage may be overcome in the future. However, if the experience of industrially developed countries of the world is any guide, a country can never have too much of managerial talent. Consequently, the move toward a national labor market is not likely to be retracted in the foreseeable future.

MANAGER IMAGE

Until after World War II industrial managers in India had no identity of their own. Those who were high on the organizational hierarchy saw themselves as extensions of owner-entrepreneurs. Many who had specialized training, as engineers, accountants, economists and lawyers, identified themselves with their respective fields of expertise. Those who had neither a specialized education nor a high rank had to be satisfied with the "head-clerk" image. There was no association of the managers and little awareness of "management" as a field of systematic study. But all this has changed very rapidly as a result of governmental initiative.

Management Education

After India attained her political independence in 1947, and when the nationalist government settled down to the task of achieving the goal of rapid industrialization, it became evident

[14] For a discussion of the international nature of this problem, see S. B. Prasad, "International Search for Managerial Talent," *Michigan Business Review*, January, 1965, pp. 9-12.

that progress in this direction would be hindered by the lack of adequate managerial talent. There were no facilities in the country for any kind of formal education and training in business or industrial management. Indeed many universities offered bachelor's and master's degrees in commerce; but these programs were so poorly conceived and organized that the employer saw no advantage in hiring the commerce graduates.[15] Faced with this situation the University Education Commission which was appointed by the Government of India in 1948 "to report on Indian university education and suggest improvements and extensions that may be desirable to suit present and future requirements of the country,"[16] recommended establishment of graduate curriculum in business administration. In December 1949 the All-India Council for Technical Education, a body appointed by the government of India to give advice on the development and coordination of technical education in the country, gave attention to the question and appointed a Committee of Industrial Administration and Business Management. This Committee was asked to examine in detail the question of education and training in industrial administration and business management and to draw up a suitable scheme of management studies. The Committee made its report in June 1953 in which it made three main recommendations: (i) An Administrative Staff College patterned after the Administrative Staff College at Henley-on-Thames in England should be established; (ii) A Board of Management Studies be set up to formulate a scheme for the development of management studies at the university level; and (iii) A National Institute of Management, patterned after the American Management Association should be created. These recommendations were accepted by the government.

The first university level program in business management was offered in 1954. By 1957 seven selected universities and similar institutions were offering these programs to those having "a Bachelor's degree in engineering, technology, commerce, arts or equivalent qualification, plus at least two years of experience in business." All but one of these programs were offered in the

---

[15] See Report of the University Education Commission, *op. cit.*, Vol. I, especially p. 207, and Report of the Special Committee for Commerce Education, *op. cit.*
[16] University Education Commission Report, *op. cit.*, p. 1.

evening on a part-time basis and it took three years to success-fully complete the program. The full-time program could be completed in one year. None of these programs led to a university degree.

At first there was a great deal of confusion regarding the purpose of these programs and the methods to be employed. This problem was further compounded by the absence of suitable faculty and teaching material. To deal with these problems, the Government of India consulted several American and British management experts and sent Indian management educators to the United States to study the organization of management education. The net result of these efforts has been twofold. First, the American model for university level education in manage-ment has been accepted. Consequently, management programs in the selected universities have been promoted to the level of "Department" which, in turn, have started offering full-time programs leading to a Master's degree in business or industrial management.

Second, two national institutes of management, named Indian Institute of Management, Calcutta and Indian Institute of Management, Ahmedabad, have been established to serve as models for management education in India, to prepare research scholars and competent teachers for universities and other insti-tutions engaged in management education, and to provide training, research and consulting services to industry and govern-ments in all matters of management. The Sloan School of Management of MIT, and the Harvard Graduate School of Business Administration are providing the technical and faculty assistance to the Calcutta and Ahmedabad Institute respectively. Neither of these institutes have come into their own yet. They started out with executive development programs in 1962, and at the time of this writing they had admitted their first group of students for an MBA level two-year program.

Administrative Staff College

In pursuance of the second recommendation of the Committee on Industrial Administration and Business Management, the Administrative Staff College of India was established at Hyder-abad, and it admitted its first group of trainees in December

1957. Organized on the model of its British counterpart, it offers three-month long residential programs for middle and upper level executives from both business and government. It admits about 50 executives in each of its three-month sessions. Its courses are taught through the "syndicate method" developed by Staff College at Henley-on-Thames.

Management Association

To implement the third recommendation of the Committee on Industrial Administration and Business Management, a sub-committee evolved the following blueprint for a national management association:

The organization should be called the Indian Management Association, and it should be established with headquarters in Delhi as a joint enterprise of the government, industry and commerce. The objectives should be to coordinate and harmonize activities of different professional institutions and organizations which are effective in their own special field, as well as organizations of broader interests which do not claim management as their primary concern, but can make a useful contribution in this field; to establish branches of the association in various parts of the country, to organize conferences both regional and national, on management; to maintain a library of management literature and prepare and publish books, papers and periodicals; to prepare films and visual aids which contribute to the understanding of management methods and techniques and current developments in this sphere; to provide an information bureau; to take a lead in management research; to maintain a liaison with universities and other educational institutions in respect of development of management education; to bring to India sound management thinking and practices from overseas and encourage and develop by all possible means such practices and standards in all walks of national life.[17]

The sub-committee report carried other details on constitution, organizational structure, grades of membership, functional relationship with other bodies, requirements of staff, finance, etc.

For reasons which are not very clear, no direct governmental action was taken to bring such an association into being. However, such a body came into being through an indirect governmental action. In 1954, the government of India had invited A. T. Kearney and Company, a firm of management consultants from Chicago, to assist in various aspects of management education. One of the assignments given to this firm was to assist in the establishment of adult education for management. In fulfillment of this assignment, the Chicago firm promoted local

[17] As reported in Report of a Visit to the United States, *op. cit.*, p. 6.

associations of management in six large cities of India. In June 1956, these local associations got together in a meeting held at Bangalore and decided to form an all-India body under the name All-India Management Association (AIMA). The main function visualized for the body was that of coordinating activities of the local groups, exchanging information and sponsoring short term training programs. In 1957, the AIMA sent a delegation to the 11th session of the International Scientific Management Congress held at Paris, and now it is its full-fledged member.

At present the AIMA has nearly a score of local affiliates whose activities include lectures, inter-plant visits, discussion groups, newsletters, short courses and institutes. The AIMA has its headquarters in New Delhi. Its most important activity is to serve as an information bureau. It publishes a monthly magazine under the title *Indian Management* which has yet to attain its stature both as a scholarly and professional publication. In addition, it publishes a quarterly bulletin which lists all management courses, seminars, and conferences to be held in India under various auspices during the next three months. In the field of management training, the AIMA's activities are very limited. Between 1957 and 1960 it sent, through the sponsorship of the Ford Foundation, twelve participants to attend the Advanced Management Program in the Far East, held in the Philippines by members of the Harvard Business School faculty. From 1960 it has been conducting a four-week summer residential course for the top management to which thirty to forty persons are admitted. Further it has undertaken responsibility for holding the Overseas Graduate Examinations of the British Institute of Management.

Complete data on the membership of the AIMA and its affiliates could not be obtained. However, the 1963 study of Indian managers showed that out of 1982 managers in the sample only 123, that is, nearly six per cent were members of AIMA local chapters.[18] Further, the AIMA and its local affiliates are for all practical purposes bodies of middle level managers. With

---

[18] Here it should be pointed out that an average Indian manager is not much of a "joiner." Fifty-two per cent did not belong to any professional or trade association. But the remaining forty-eight per cent belonged to 1.8 organizations on the average. There were no significant differences among the four generations of managers on this account.

a few notable exceptions, the top level managers are not very active in these organizations. One plausible reason for this phenomenon could be that middle management people have a greater need to discover and establish their occupational identity than the people at the top who have a fairly well established identity as owners, entrepreneurs or employers. A membership in management association can be particularly reassuring to those managers who lack an alternate "respectable" identity, like that of an engineer. Another contributory factor may be the fact that industrial employers in India have a long history of having a tarnished image. Their single-minded pursuit of profit has a lot to do with it. As a result of widespread profiteering and black marketing during World War II, the industrialists added a few rather ugly scars to their already unpopular image.[19] A lot of middle level managers not associated with decision-making functions of the companies, did not want any part of this image. They needed an identity apart from their employers, and they are finding it by belonging to the AIMA.

Other Governmental Initiative

During the last decade the Government of India has initiated several other programs for improving the training and skills of the managers. Here the following need special mention:

[19] The widespread public hostility toward businessmen in India during the period immediately after the war is shown in the following remarks of Prime Minister Nehru. Addressing the Tripartite Industries Conference in New Delhi on December 18, 1947, he said:

"As far as the employer's side is concerned, I hope no one will challenge me when I say that during this last War a certain section of the employer class did not behave well; in fact they behaved exceedingly badly, exceedingly egotistically and far from giving a square deal to anybody, they thought mostly of themselves and of little else...we have to find some means and machinery to prevent this kind of shameful traffic in human beings and profiting at the expense of the nation." (Jawaharlal Nehru, *Independence and After, A Collection of Speeches 1946-49.* New York: John Day Co., 1950, p. 149) Again in a speech delivered at the meeting of the Federation of Indian Chambers of Commerce and Industry, held in New Delhi on March 4, 1949, he said:

"Whatever the rights and wrongs of things may be, the industrialists and the commercial classes in India have become unpopular with the general mass of the people. They have become unpopular because some people amongst them have not behaved rightly, have taken advantage of situation to obtain profit for themselves at an inordinate rate to the disadvantage of the community at large." (*Ibid.,* p. 193).

For an illustration of some of these malpractices, see *Report of the Commission of Inquiry (Inquiry on the Administration of Dalmia-Jain Companies)*, Government of India, Ministry of Commerce and Industry, Department of Company Law Administration, Delhi, 1963.

1. TWI CENTER: Training Within Industry (TWI) Scheme is intended primarily for lower level managers and supervisors. Introduced in 1950 on an experimental basis with the help of the I.L.O.'s Asian Field Office on Technical Training, the Government of India was so impressed by the effect of TWI programs on productivity that it decided to set up a TWI center to promote such training in all sectors of industry. This center was established in 1954 as a unit in the Central Labor Institute – an institution set up by the Ministry of Labour.

2. NATIONAL PRODUCTIVITY COUNCIL: Established in 1958 at the insistence of the Government of India and with support from the U.S. Government, the National Productivity Council is an autonomous organization registered as a "society." Its stated purposes are "to stimulate productivity consciousness in the country and to provide services with a view to maximizing the utilization of available resources of men, machines, materials and power, to Wage War against Waste; to help secure for the people of the country a better and higher standard of living."[20] To this end, the Council collects and disseminates information about techniques and procedures of productivity, conducts training programs for various levels of management, sends productivity teams to various countries to study and report on different aspects of problems in specific industries.

3. SMALL INDUSTRIES SERVICE INSTITUTES: Aware of the important role that small-scale industries can play in the economic development of the country, the Government of India has given special attention to their growth and development beginning with the First Five Year Plan. Several administrative and organizational measures have been taken in this regard. Among them is the establishment of a network of Small Industries Service Institutes and Extension Centers which are manned by a corps of technical and specialized personnel. Now an institution on the lines of Indian Institutes of Management has been established to train personnel for various positions of responsibility in the field of small-scale industries.

4. INDUSTRIAL RESEARCH ASSOCIATIONS: The Government of India has encouraged industries by providing tax exemptions

[20] From an introductory statement on the National Productivity Council of India in *Productivity, Journal of NPC*, Vol. 1, No. 4 (April-May, 1960).

and annual subsidies to organize cooperative research associations. Three such associations have been established. They are the Ahmedabad Textile Industry Research Association (ATIRA) Bombay Textile Research Association (BTRA), and South India Textile Research Association (SITRA). These associations have done some pioneering work in management and supervisory training. The contributions of the ATIRA, oldest of the three, have been most notable.

Non-Governmental Initiatives

The post-independence ferment in the field of management development and training in India has caused people outside the government to take notice of the situation. This in turn led to other developments. Several employers have set up their own management development programs and have hired full-time staff for this purpose.[21] Nearly a dozen management consulting firms have come into being. Most of these firms offer services for recruitment, selection and training of supervisory and managerial personnel. Further, some of the older special-interest associations, like the Indian Institute of Personnel Management, have become considerably more active than ever before.

Management Pool

Facing the problem of inadequate supply of managers for manning the public sector enterprises, the Government of India decided to establish an Industrial Management Service on the lines similar to those for the Indian Administrative Service. Recruitment to this service was visualized to be made from within the other "services" as well as from outside.[22]

The initial decision to create an Industrial Management Service and the later decision to establish the "Management Pool" may have done more for the image of Indian managers than any other official or non-official action. For these actions amount to putting the manager on an equal footing with the career civil servant who enjoys a very high occupational status in India.

---

[21] The exact number of such firms is not known. On the basis of an educated guess the number may be around twenty.

[22] See Chapter 7 for a discussion of the "Industrial Management Pool."

Is the Indian Manager Becoming Professionalized?

Now we have the essential data to answer this question. Let us take our four attributes of profession and examine these data in their light.

Until a decade ago "management" was not recognized as a field of systematic learning and training in India. Facing the problem of finding increasing numbers of managerial personnel for implementing its industrialization plans, the government of India came to accept that "management" could be taught like medicine, law and engineering. With this acceptance, the Government has moved to create a variety of teaching and training facilities in this field. These facilities have been established by borrowing the knowledge, teaching and training methods as well as teaching personnel from countries like the United States and Britain which have a fairly long history of management education. The governmental initiative in this regard has been followed up by employers and other interested people. As a result of these newly created training facilities, the proportion of those with some formal education and training in management has been increasing. However, such persons are still in a minority. More important than this is the fact that an entry into management is not subject to a formal education and training in this field.[23] Nor is a formal training in management a guarantee for entry into management. Further, there is no reliable evidence that graduates of "management courses" enjoy any preferential treatment either at the time of hiring or at some later stage of their career. In fact, many people have serious doubts that a graduate in management would make a better manager than somebody else having the same amount of education in some other field. These doubts seem to have two main roots:

First, it is believed, rightly or wrongly, that a successful manager is basically a personality type. A person with the necessary personality make-up can be taught the management "know-how"; but little can be done with a person who has the know-how but lacks the necessary personality qualities.[24] Such

---

[23] It should be pointed out that such a practice is not peculiar to India, but is found widely throughout the world including countries like the United States and Britain from where most management training programs have been imported by India.

[24] The writings on the subject are plentiful. For a useful annotated bibliography

a belief finds support in the fact that many well-known people in the field of management in India and abroad never had any formal training in management.

Secondly, often there is no sharp distinction made between managerial and engineering-technical jobs. A production manager of a plant may be both a production-engineer and a manager at the same time. Similarly the top man in the research division of a company may be both a working scientist and the manager of the division. Under these circumstances, the employers tend to attach primary importance to the "technical-scientific" knowledge and give only secondary consideration to the "management" knowledge.

Although a formal training in management is not given a great deal of importance in the hiring of the manager, four to six years of college education have become almost a universal prerequisite for entry into Indian management. Considering the facts regarding the very low literacy of the Indian population and the correspondingly low education of the average industrial worker in India, a college educated manager is likely to be considered a more knowledgeable person. Despite this, he is not likely to enjoy an expert status accorded to, say, a doctor or a lawyer. A professional's superior knowledge and skills are recognized universally. But there will be many who will challenge a college graduate's views on what, why and how of management.

The Indian manager is getting increasingly conscious of his identity as a "manager." This consciousness has been largely forced upon him by circumstances beyond his control. Until the end of World War II there was considerable confusion regarding the role, function and status of managers of business and industrial enterprises in India. Their identity was often submerged in the identities of other groups. But when, after independence, the government of India decided to accelerate the industrialization process, the resultant shortage of managerial manpower caused the government and the public to give considerable attention to several questions concerning the role, function, training and the status of "managers." All this attention has established a separate identity of managers. Further, as a critical talent for industriali-

of research writings see Robert A. Gorden and James E. Howell, *Higher Education for Business* (New York: Columbia University Press, 1958), Appendix I.

zation, they have been accorded a status comparable with those of established civil and administrative services and professions. These developments have come so fast that they may have left many a manager as well as others around them a bit dizzy. But on the whole these changes have gone over well.

To consolidate their recent gains of identity and high status, the Indian managers have established the All-India Management Association with local chapters in all major industrial cities. Many managers are also active in Productivity Councils and TWI Associations. However, the activities of all these associations are almost entirely devoted to skill improvement. Little or no attention is given to other aspects of managerial behavior. These associations set no standards and have no police functions. Also an advancement in the hierarchy of these associations is not a matter of great prestige.

The circumstances which have caused the Indian managers to come into their present status have also emphasized their social role, namely, they are responsible for the industrial development as well as for the larger well-being of the society. However, there are few systematic data regarding the extent of Indian managers' commitment to this role. Indeed, there is no paucity of formal pronouncements by individuals and groups of managers which would lead to a belief that they are aware of public expectations of them. But what importance they attach to community interests vis-à-vis their own self-interest is a matter of debate and speculation. Managers have no established code of ethics to guide their behavior in relation to those with whom they serve and deal. They have no device for selfpolicing except their own conscience and fear of possible trouble with law. On the basis of the fact that an increasing number of managers are coming from professional families, it may be argued that their upbringing is so molding their superegos as to make them properly attuned to public well-being. But, then, such an argument is mostly in the realm of hoping. Even this hope loses some ground when it is remembered that the managers show an increasing tendency to begin their careers with a managerial or a similarly well-placed position. Having been born and brought up in *elite* families, and having started their career near the top, they may have little empathy with the proverbial "man-in-the-street," and with his hopes and expectations. In the absence of such empathy, they may behave and act in a fashion which would inadvertently result in unfairness to the well-being of the larger society.

Bureaucratization was suggested as a fourth attribute of a profession. Indian management has achieved a lot in this direction. Indeed favoritism and nepotism have not been altogether rooted out. But today a son of the manager does not inherit his father's position as he inherits his property. Nor are people hired into managerial positions primarily because of their religion, caste or regional origin. If these factors are given any consideration, it is only after their job merit has been established.

Conclusion

The last decade has seen the Indian manager emerging with an identity of his own and gaining a status of high prestige. Also with the passing of years, Indian management has become increasingly bureaucratized. However, any further advance to ward professionalization of the Indian manager depends upon two factors: one, advances in the systematized and generalized knowledge in the field of management, which in turn would generate greater confidence among the employers about the superiority of those who possess such knowledge; and two, evolution of standards of behavior which would guide a manager in dealings with others. In the meanwhile, the Indian managers should be happy about recent improvements in their status, and should be modest in pressing their claim to a "professional" status.

CHAPTER 4

RELEVANCE OF WESTERN THEORIES

Perhaps the most revolutionary change in the modern civilization started with the so-called Industrial Revolution which got underway in the western world and is now spreading to the "underdeveloped countries" of Asia, Africa, and South America which by any definition still comprise about $\frac{3}{4}$ of the world's population. "Technology" can be regarded as the main outcome of the Industrial Revolution.[1] In an anthropological sense "technology" can be construed as a vital aspect of culture. Then of all aspects of *culture* such as social organization, religion, art, and philosophy, it has been technology from which elements have been most readily diffused from one country to another or from one society to another. This diffusion has been facilitated by at least three factors. The first is the conducive "environment" or set of values (or the scientific or sociological basis); the second is the fact that technological elements are more amenable to objective, comparative evaluations than are the elements from other aspects of *culture*. Thus in a society which has been exposed to a new tool, technique, or knowhow, people can make reasonably fair evaluations of the advantages of adopting it. Such is not the case, for instance, when a new art style or motif has been introduced in an alien society.

[1] What is this technology or technological progress which has been the cause of rising income and output? Everett E. Hagen provides an excellent explanation thus: "In essence it consists of two steps: the discovery of new knowledge which makes possible an increase in the output of goods and services per unit of labor, capital, and materials used in production; and the incorporation of that knowledge in the productive processes. It includes the devising of more satisfying products as well as more efficient methods of production. It includes the entire process of innovation, from an advance in pure science to its adaptation in engineering and its application in production. Within the realm of methods it includes not only scientific and technical advances but also the devising of new forms of organization or methods of procedure which make the society more efficient in production. To term all these somewhat varied activities "technological progress" is not to use the term as a catchall. They have in common the devising of new concepts, which is the essence of technological progress." See Everett E. Hagen, *On the Theory of Social Change* (Homewood, Illinois: The Dorsey Press, Inc., 1962), pp. 11-12.

The third factor, as described by the anthropologist, Ralph Linton, is that techniques and material products emanating in one *culture* can be easily transmitted to another *culture* because they are most readily and completely expressed for an alien observer.

It is the second factor which, to the greatest extent, tends to facilitate the intercultural exchange of technological elements and continues to play a paramount role in the spread of the twentieth century Western *culture* throughout many parts of the world today. An extremely significant part of Western technology is *Management Know-how*. The broad question relating to transmission of management technology and determination of the relevance and applicability of American management know-how among Indian industrial firms is the subject of the ensuing chapter.

The economic development of the "advanced" countries such as the United States and the United Kingdom during the past two centuries would not have been possible without the acquisition of an improving technology and also the progressive creation of organizations necessary for the practical application of such technology to derive its benefits. The theme of this chapter is the relevance and applicability to two sets of "management-organization" theories, which have evolved in the western context and which have provided the building blocks for the organizations through which the benefits of technology have been derived, in the Indian context.

The purpose of this chapter is twofold: first, to examine the essence of the western management-organization theories and briefly explore the nature of public enterprises in India with a view to setting up a general frame of reference; and second, to examine the issues of relevance and applicability as well as usefulness of two sets of hypotheses relating to goal-setting, and decision-making in the context of public enterprise organizations in India. The tenor of the chapter is theoretical and comparative rather than empirical.

Some definitions and assumptions

The following terms employed in this chapter are operationally defined or identified as follows:

1. *Culture.* This sonorous term is operationally defined as the composite of artifacts, attitudes, mores, and prevailing technology as they can be identified in one geographic boundary, among one group of people, or within a political entity. It is implied that what we generally refer to as "technology" is part and parcel of culture identified as above and is the most amenable aspect of culture to change through transformation and transmission. Furthermore, managerial systems are regarded as part of a given technology.

2. *Management-Organization Theories.* A theory is composed of both systematic and doctrinal elements which are embedded in its language, logic, and normative considerations. Since there is, as yet, no unified organizational theory from which principles of effective management can be deduced, and since hunches, hypotheses, and partial theories are employed to describe, explain, and predict business behavior or the behavior of managers, the general term "management-organization theories" is used in this chapter. The two sets of hypotheses or theories which are examined in this chapter are those which relate to goal-setting, and decision-making.

3. *Western.* By Western, reference is here made to the United States predominantly. Many elements of the managerial-organizational theories emerged in the expositions of Frederick Taylor, Mary Parker Follett, Elton Mayo, and Chester Barnard in the United States. Some significant contributions from abroad have also been made to this area, for example, Henri Fayol's expositions from France and Colonel Lyndall Urwick's contributions from Great Britain, but by and large, Western refers to the American contributors cited above as well as to the contributions made during the last decade or so by Richard Cyert, James March, Herbert Simon and others.

4. *Relevance-Applicability.* Relevance means "to have a bearing upon," as for example, the Indian context. Although in a dictionary sense, applicability is a synonym to relevance, the term applicability is meant to convey the notion of workability. For example, the concept of "democratic management" may be relevant to a factory in India but it may not be applicable in the sense that workers may not be ready or may even be unwilling to participate in the decision-making process. Where people are

largely illiterate, but not necessarily unintelligent, and where they have been conditioned to authority, authoritarian measures may be more workable than democratic ones.

Since the chapter essentially deals with theories in the context of developing India, it is apt also to make some assumptions regarding the context. These are general assumptions.

1. Any proposed solution to the problem of economic development[2] necessarily embodies both a theory and a strategy. While the theory identifies the variables that determine the rate of development, the strategy proposes the mechanisms by which the variables are to be altered. With respect to developmental strategy, one of the major problems is to determine to what degree the others' experience is applicable, that is, whether remedies which worked in other countries can, with necessary adjustments, be transferred and adapted.

2. A significant problem in formulating strategies is to build necessary organizations. Technological progress depends upon teamwork and proper organization. Organization is a complement to rather than a substitute for other factors of production. In other words, it is not enough to say that growth is a function of land, capital, labor and engineering technology. There must be an element which combines these in the right proportions, sets the manifold tasks, and sees to their accomplishment.[3]

3. The instrument of industrial production on any important scale in a developing country is inevitably the corporate organization, private, or public. The effectiveness of these organizations, in terms of the goals defined for it, depends upon more efficient use of existing equipment, materials, and labor as well as upon improvement of the existing management talents. There is a marked difference among administrative abilities, engineer-

[2] Maurice Zinkin in his book *Development of Free Asia* emphasized nearly a decade ago that economic development is the pursuit of rising standards of material welfare rather than increasing happiness. He also pleads for a rational pursuit of the development objectives, with the rate of return as the central criterion of allocative decisions – this rate in turn being conceived within the context of a social rather than private cost-benefit calculus.

[3] As Lord Lionel Robbins recently expressed it, "We do not need economic analysis to tell us that a country with a fertile soil, good climate and extensive mineral resources has a better chance of economic development than the one which is not so placed. What needs to be said, however, is that it is not sufficient for these resources to be physically present; they have to be known and used – which brings us at once to the functions of management." See his talk reported in *Advanced Management Journal*, (July, 1965, p. 24).

ing skills, and managerial talents. Management both at the policy-level and the execution-level constitutes one of the most important instruments for the development strategy of a country.

Summing up, then, the general assumption in this chapter is that the corporate form of organization is inevitable in India, and with due emphasis upon management and organization, the effectiveness of these enterprises can be enhanced and their contributions to economic development optimized.

With a brief characterization of public enterprises in India, the discussion in this chapter pertains first to the essence of Western management-organization theories, and second to the theories of goal-setting and decision-making in terms of their relevance, applicability to public enterprises in India.

The Public Enterprise in India: A brief characterization

While purely economic considerations are vital, public enterprises in India are not just business enterprises in the sense in which it is understood by private businessmen. There is a certain philosophy behind the extension of India's public sector. This philosophy is one of democratic socialism. The professed aim is to use the public sector as a major instrument for bringing into existence and operating a democratic socialist society. As a country India is committed to a policy of achieving a part of her industrial and economic development by means of public sector enterprises.

The majority of public enterprises have been established as companies under the Companies Act. Nevertheless these enterprises are susceptible to the environmental influences of a planned economy as well as parliamentary interference and control.

Public sector enterprises are immense undertakings and have come to stay in India. They are also growing in size and stature. If the fourth Five-Year Plan estimates prove true, at the end of the Fourth-Plan period the public sector in organized industry and commerce would have a capital base of no less than $10 billion. Thus the public sector enterprises constitute the most significant sector of the Indian economy.

In general, the situation thus far in the public sector, especially in the area of industrial and mineral development would suggest that the majority of public sector projects have taken longer to complete, benefits from them have come in later than expected, and the majority of the projects have cost the country more than originally estimated. In a word they have been less effective than originally planned.

The concept of effectiveness in the public sector enterprises fundamentally relates to means, and not to ends, since ends are subject to political decisions, either by the ministers or the parliamentary body.

The public enterprises face some unique problems. They are exposed to public criticism, sometimes rightly as in regard to corruption.[4] The repercussions of such criticism have been two-fold: a weakening of the will to make bold decisions on the part of enterprise managers, and an intruding tendency on the part of the ministries. There is also the difficult problem of reconciling managerial initiative and autonomy with ministerial account-ability to Parliament.

In essence, then, the large complex public sector industrial organizations are new to the Indian economic environment and the issues of the effectiveness of these organizations are of quite pivotal importance in any consideration of economic develop-ment – a subject of the most vivid contemporary interest. It should be recognized that these issues are by no means simple and few. Among the multifarious issues that have a bearing upon the effectiveness of large complex organizations, from the point of view of theory, only two aspects will be dealt with in the following discussions. To reiterate, they relate to goal-setting and decision-making.

Essence of Western Management-Organization Theories

Management-organization theories and research in this area are prominently culture-bound. This is the conclusion which Bertram M. Gross reached after an examination of some six hundred studies.[5] More than ninety per cent of the studies

---

[4] The following is an interesting recent comment made by an Indian author: "Corruption in the public services is a complex phenomenon. It has sociological, economic, ethico-religious, administrative, juristic, and even political roots. All these facts must be taken into account in any attempt to tackle this problem." See P. S. Muhr, "Corruption in the Public Services in India," *Indian Journal of Political Science*, Volume XXVI, Number 1, (January-March, 1965), p. 3.

[5] Bertram M. Gross, *The Managing of Organizations*, Vol. II (New York: The Free Press of Glencoe, 1964), p. 894.

which Gross evaluated dealt with organizations of one type or another in the United States. There were a few exceptions – comparative studies.[6] Some, but not many, steps have been undertaken to escape this insularity. In public administration and in business administration one can delineate a few studies which deal with the socioeconomic environment and make cross-cultural comparisons. Besides, there is a tremendous need for more intra-cultural studies, too.

If we can identify the management-organization theories as being culturebound, then, a basic question may be raised: *What are the essential features of these culture-bound management-organization theories?*

These theories are recent. They are progressing beyond the methodological stage of armchair theorizing and casual empiricism. Of course, organizations are not something new in human history. They are as old as mankind. However, attention was centered on management-organization theories as a distinctive discipline of thought only at the beginning of the current century with the so-called "scientific management" movement. The analysts of the first quarter of the twentieth century with their contributions to the theory and practice of scientific management brought new hope for better living by increasing productivity through "scientific" development of the efficiency of the organization. The idea of efficiency provided a unifying theme in the work of early pioneers. The organization scientism – meaning that the same techniques which have worked out well in the physical sciences are likely to lead to the development of an exact science of man – marked the new era in technological progress through scientific development of organized effort.

While the organizational thinking of the first quarter of the twentieth century was clear-cut and imbedded with the so-called classical principles of management-organization, the second quarter marked an era of skepticism. This doubt took various forms. First, the Hawthorne studies disclosed that human beings were not merely instruments of production and that human productivity was not merely a simple mechanistic procedure but

---

[6] For example, see Stephen A. Richardson, "Organizational Contrasts on British and American Ships," *Administrative Science Quarterly*, Vol. I, 1956-57, pp. 189-207. Albert Lauterbach, "Perceptions of Management: Case Materials from Western and Northern Europe," *Administrative Science Quarterly*, Vol. II, 1957, pp. 97-109.

a complex socio-psychological process. Second, a number of social scientists realized that organizations were not isolated or closed systems functioning independently of their environment but they were parts of a broader social system – the society.

In the light of these findings a metamorphosis of management-organization theories has occurred. The borders of these theories have been extended. The observational basis for theorizing is much stronger than before. Organizational analysis has become an inter-disciplinary (or multi-disciplinary) concern. It is still in ferment. There is little by way of convergence, or by way of synthesis. Nevertheless one can discern three central tendencies in the management-organization theories.

Three Central Tendencies

Organizations are complex multi-dimensional social systems and they should be studied as such.

The new dimensions and perspectives in studying organizational complexity need new tools and techniques of analysis. There are various methods and models exemplifying these.

Beyond the methodological diversification there is no common agreement on the orientation, perspectives, and philosophical foundation of organizational thought although now and then there is a plea for a satisfactory synthesis or fusion which is seldom translated into action. Basically one can delineate two major schools of thought:

1. Defending the traditional managerial principles emphasizing formal authority, hierarchy, and organizational structure.

2. Tending to repudiate these and stressing the so-called social character of organization, placing more attention on group processes, informal organization, and the socio-psychological factors of managerial-organizational behavior.

Basic Frames of Reference and Perspectives

Amidst the diversity of ideas as they relate to the study of large organizations, one can also discern several basic frames of reference and perspectives as recorded in the current literature. A few of these culturebound perspectives are relevant to the Indian context and may be identified as such.

1. *Organization as a product of historical development:* This frame

of reference is based upon the premise that there exist a close relationship between the present and the past. This relationship offers a basis for understanding the present and predicting the future by analyzing the trends revealed in the study of the past. This frame of reference as employed in the explorations of such authors as Beard, Gaus, Macmahon, Mansfield, Waldo and White[7] may not be relevant to the Indian context in question since most public sector organizations are post-1947 phenomena. There is not much historical relationship between other forms of governmental undertakings and the modern large-scale industrial enterprises in the public sector.

2. *Organization as a societal phenomenon*: This approach views organizations as parts of man's social setting or as social institutions conditioned by the forces which dominate society as one complex entity. This frame of reference as found in the explanations of Clemmer, Mayo, Miller and Form, Selznick, Warner, and Weber[8] is quite relevant to the Indian context since public enterprise organizations can be construed as socialist-societal phenomena. A variant of this approach places special emphasis on cultural differences and ecology as, for example, illustrated in the works of Gardner and Moore, and Malinowski.[9]

3. *Organization as an organic system*: In this approach organizations are analyzed and described in terms analogous to the organic body or as an entity in itself different and distinct from its component parts. Follett, McCurdy, Miller and many researchers at the University of Michigan use this perspective.[10]

4. *Organization as a system of cooperative action*: This is the frame of reference one finds in the work of Chester Barnard, and some

[7] See Dwight Waldo, *Perspectives of Administration* (University: University of Alabama Press, 1956), especially pp. 50-76 for elaboration of the works of these authors.

[8] See Donald Clemmer, *The Prison Community* (Boston, 1940); Elton Mayo, *The Social Problems of Industrial Civilization* (Boston, 1945); Delbert Miller and W. H. Form, *Industrial Sociology* (New York, 1951); Philip Selznick, *Leadership in Administration* (Evanston, Ill., 1957); W. L. Warner and O. Low, *The Social System of the Modern Factory* (New Haven, 1947); for a statement of Max Weber's thesis see Rober K. Merton, *et al. Reader in Bureaucracy* (Glencoe, Ill., 1952.)

[9] Burleigh Gardner and D. G. Moore, *Human Relations in Industry* (Chicago, 1950); B. Malinowski, *A Scientific Theory of Culture and Other Essays* (Chapel Hill, 1944), and *The Dynamics of Culture Change* (New Haven, 1945).

[10] Mary P. Follett's papers were edited by Metcalf and Urwick and published as *Dynamic Administration, the Collected Papers of Mary Parker Follett* (New York, 1941); John MacCurdy, *The Structure of Morale* (Cambridge, 1943); for an account of the University of Michigan studies, see Harry Goode, "Greenhouses of Science for Management," *Management Science*, July, 1958.

of the works of Herbert Simon.[11] This frame of reference may be relevant to the entire societal phenomenon in the democratic-socialist India but may not be relevant to industrial organizations such as public sector enterprises.

5. *Organization as an intermediate phenomenon:* According to this approach there are three levels of multi-person units: the primary group, the institution, and, somewhere in between these two, the organizations. This perspective is recorded in the works of Dahl and Lindblom, Dill, and also Herbert Simon.[12]

6. *Organization as crossroads of individual and collective behavior:* This is the frame of reference of the "fusion theorists" such as Chris Argyris and E. Wight Bakke.[13] Confronted with the basic problems of organization and management as they are, the public enterprise organizations in India at the present time are likely to derive little, if any, benefit from the so-called fusion theory.

7. *Organization as a production system or a man-machine interface:* In this frame of reference, organization is a production system or the structuring of individuals, functions, and resources into productive relationships. This frame of reference is universally applicable although variance can be found in the proportion of the man and machine component of the production systems. This frame of reference is prominent in the field of administration and management, that is administering the activities of an organization and managing an organization. The basic concern of this approach is about the nature of the organization as a goal-accomplishing organization and the conditions under which its structure and functions contribute to accomplishment of these goals efficiently and effectively. Within this broad frame of reference, central to which is the model of business or industrial enterprise, at least five methods of analysis can be traced in current literature in management and organization. They are:

[11] Chester Barnard, *The Functions of the Executive* (1938) and *Organization and Management* (1948); Herbert Simon, *Administrative Behavior* (New York: 1954.)

[12] Robert Dahl and C. E. Lindblom, *Politics, Economics and Welfare* (New York, 1953); W. R. Dill, "Environment as an Influence of Managerial Autonomy," *Administrative Science Quarterly*, March 1958; H. A. Simon, *Administrative Behavior* (1954).

[13] Chris Argyris, *The Present State of Human Relations Research* (1953), *Personality and Organization* (1957), *Integrating the Individual and the Organization* (1964); E. Wight Bakke, *Bonds of Organization* (1950), *The Individual and the Organization* (1951), etc.

descriptive of the structure and functions of the organizations; *analytical*, in the sense of searching for the underlying reasons for identifiable organizational behavior or more precisely behavior of members in an organization; *pragmatic*, that is, directed toward the study of conditions under which an organization develops to its highest degree of efficiency and effectiveness; *normative*, that is, seeking to lay down the standards or norms of ideal management of administrative structure, thought and behavior; and *philosophical*, that is, attempting to articulate the perspective of management-organization theory with the philosophical foundations of making or trying to integrate the phenomenon of organizational behavior with the generic process of human existence.

These five approaches are not, of course, clear-cut and distinctive in current literature but they represent more or less the characteristic trends of the culture-bound management-organization theories. Although many researchers and writers in the West have construed these approaches to be distinct, it is more useful and challenging to regard them as sequences in the scientific inquiry of organization in the Indian context – the administered society, than as separate approaches. Parenthetically, it may be noted that, for example, if one were to embark upon empirical studies of industrial organizations in the public sector, the following descriptive model could be used.

Diagram 1.

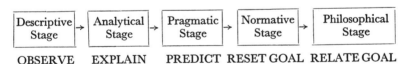

Descriptive Stage	Analytical Stage	Pragmatic Stage	Normative Stage	Philosophical Stage
OBSERVE	EXPLAIN	PREDICT	RESET GOAL	RELATE GOAL

Of all the seven basic frames of reference or perspectives cited above, the last one, namely organization as production system appears to be most applicable to the Indian context. It is within this frame of reference that two aspects of management-organization theories – goal-setting and decision-making theories – will be examined in the following discussion.

The most fundamental feature of the organization is not that it simply is made up of people, or that it is a cooperative system, a decision unit or an organic whole – as useful as these theoretical perspectives may be, but it is a system within which work is done by people and machines. This work is fundamentally the transformation of inputs into outputs. Goals of an organization set limits upon the type of work and decisions facilitate achievement of goals.

Goal Setting: Theory and Relevance

There are perhaps two classic ways of theorizing in economics in a broad sense concerning goals and goal-setting in industrial organizations. One is to describe the organization as consisting of, or tantamount to, an entrepreneur, and then defining the goal of the organization as the goal of the entrepreneur. Of course, the entrepreneur under contemporary conditions may very well refer to the top of the managerial hierarchy or even a control group such as the stockholders. The second way is to theorize in terms of a consensual goal such as public welfare, common interest, general good.

In contradistinction to this economic approach, the so-called behavioral approach theorizes goals as the result of a continuous bargaining-learning process. Cyert and March, the exponents of such a view, for example, have argued that the goals of a business firm are a series of more or less independent constraints imposed on the organization through a process of bargaining among potential coalition members and elaborated overtime in response to short-run pressures.[14]

Supposing the above two distinct but related approaches are viewed as one approach, then it opens up possibilities for raising several interesting questions bearing upon the goal or goals of public enterprises in India. For example, for purposes of theoretical exposition, one can ask:

1. Can a public enterprise organization be meaningfully described as consisting of an entrepreneurial group? 2. If so, would the goal of the group be analogous to the goal of the organization?

If one were to attempt to equate the group goal and the enterprise goal, then one has to say that the entrepreneurial

---

[14] Richard M. Cyert and James G. March, *A Behavioral Theory of the Firm*, (Englewood Cliffs, N.J.: Prentice-Hall, Inc., 1963), Chapter 3.

group (or the top management group) has a goal such as profit-maximizing (or profit-satisfying) and that this is the goal of the public enterprise. By the same token, one may also have to state that, since the public enterprise is publicly owned, the control group is other than the stockholders' group in the ordinary sense. This other group, let us say the legislator's group, may have a goal – a consensual goal – such as public welfare which may be consistent with the overall philosophy of socialist societal goals. However, *prima facie*, the entrepreneurial goal would appear to be in dissonance with the legislators' goal. A conflict and its resolution become imminent.

Current discussions among scholars, economists, and managers in India strongly suggest that considerable argument is put forth nowadays in India in favor of entrepreneurial goal(s). Consider, for example, the advocacy of no less an authority than Professor V.K.R.V. Rao. That public enterprises should play their part in the generation of profits is the central theme of Rao's arguments. He has argued:

Public enterprises must be carried on a profit-making basis, not only in the sense public enterprises must yield an economic price...but must also get for the community sufficient resources for financing a part of investment and maintenance of expenditure for government... No profit, no loss in public enterprises is particularly inconsistent with a socialist economy.[15] The above excerpts suggest that not only does Rao argue for a well-defined profit function for public enterprises but also a definition of the role of profits. Recent arguments even in a communist country such as the U.S.S.R. similarly define the role of profits.[16]

[15] V. K. R. V. Rao, "The Role of Public Enterprises in the Indian Economy," *Indian Journal of Public Administration*, Vol. X, No. 3, July-Sept., 1964, p. 451. For an excellent account of the profit policy of public enterprises, see V. V. Ramanadham, *The Structure of Public Enterprise in India*, (New York: Asia Publishing House, 1961) Chapter 3, pp. 85-116.

[16] The following are excerpts from a letter written by Professor Evsei Liberman to *Time*, March 5, 1965, and produced here with the permission of Professor Liberman: "In reality the notion of profit in the Soviet economy has existed for a long time...Denial of profit by socialism and recognition of profit by capitalism has never served as the feature distinguishing socialism from capitalism. The difference is in the way profit is formed, appropriated and used...Under conditions of a planned economy, profit can and must express actual efficiency of methods of production..."
Similar arguments in favor of a profit goal in the sense of entrepreneurial goal for the public enterprises in India can be discerned in such statements as, for example, "Profitability is one way to measure the effectiveness of an undertaking in the industrial field; we must expect public sector corporations not only to perform their

In terms of the theory cited, entrepreneurial goals in terms of profit-making are highly relevant to public enterprises. The consensual goals such as public welfare, common interest, and so forth need not be neglected when the goal is set as profit.

The behavioral theory which posits goal-setting as a bargaining process among coalition members may be relevant if coalition is defined as one between the entrepreneurial group and the legislators' group. However, goal-setting as a learning process becomes meaningful if such learning is related to the experience of the so-called public enterprises in various countries. The Soviet Union and the Comecon countries have had longer experience with the process of goal-setting, and, as most students of economics and business who are familiar with current happenings in these countries know, goals are now being redefined in terms of profits. Thus the learning process of these nations and their experiences strongly suggest that the economic criterion is the best one to rely upon. The following simplified diagrammatic model is a modification of the western theories of goals and goal-setting in so far as they are relevant to the Indian context.

Diagram 2.

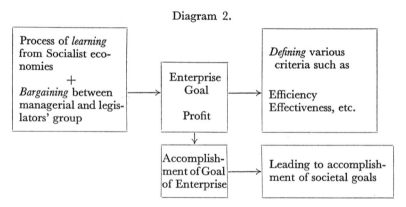

Decision-making: Theory and Relevance

At the nineteenth International Management Conference (1965), Lord Lionell Robbins made a succinct remark on the theory of decision-making, as follows: "The so-called theory of

functions of developing the country's industrial capacity but to earn a profit on our investment." These are from various sources from the *Indian Journal of Public Administration*, Vol. 10, No. 3, July-Sept. 1964.

decision-making is not a theory of ultimate decision-making but rather a theory of how to bring into proper relation the elements in decisions which are susceptible to quantitative evaluation."[17] Although various writers with various backgrounds stress decision-making as the core of managing, as management *per se*, as management science, as industrial engineering, as a statistical tool, and so forth, at best, it could be simply viewed as the process or the procedures by which the managers or executives make decisions on resource allocation. Cyert and March[18] have developed four relational concepts (quasi resolution of conflict, uncertainty avoidance, problemistic search, and organizational learning) which seem fundamental to an understanding of the decision-making process in a modern, large-scale business or industrial organization. On the basis of Lord Robbins' observation and the theoretical framework of Cyert and March, the theory of decision-making is construed here as the theory of the decision-making process and this is relevant to the large-scale public enterprises.

Herbert Simon uses "decision-making" as though it were synonymous with "managing." Even then, he views decision-making as not merely the final act of choice among alternatives but rather the whole process of decision-making. Thus, according to Simon, the decision-making process comprises three principal phases: finding occasions for making a decision; finding possible courses of action; and choosing among courses of action.[19]

Without going into the details of the traditional and the newer techniques employed in each of these three principal phases of the decision-making process of which Simon provides an excellent account, some observations on the decision-making process in the public sector enterprises can be made with a view to identifying the decision-making process in public enterprises.

Some Observations on the Decision-Process in Public Enterprises

It was noted earlier that the majority of public enterprises have been established under the Companies Act. The Joint

[17] Lord Lionell Charles Robbins, "The Role of Management in Economic Development," *Advanced Management Journal*, Volume 30, Number 3, July, 1965, p. 31.
[18] Cyert and March, *op. cit.*, pp. 116-125.
[19] Herbert Simon, *The New Science of Management Decision* (New York: Harper & Brothers Publishers, 1960), p. 1.

Stock Company form has been extensively used for the organization of manufacturing activity in the public sector in recent times in India. In 1960 there were 45 companies exclusively or partly owned by the central government and 74 companies predominantly owned by the state governments.

The joint stock form of company differs from the enterprise administered by a governmental department (e.g., Damodar Valley Corporation, Industrial Finance Corporation) in being a legal-corporate entity and possessing "autonomy" in decision-making.[20] Just what this "autonomy" is at the top managerial level is extremely hard to discern. Although the joint stock form company in the public sector is supposed to be autonomous like a British or an American private corporation, there is fundamentally a reversal of the basic philosophy implicit in the corporate organization. The corporate directors, in theory and in practice, should represent the owners of the corporations. However, the members of the corporation board in the case of the type of public enterprises in India are chosen by the government (being the owner) for their directorial abilities and not to carry out any owner-oriented mandates. The directors of these joint stock forms of governmental enterprises stand more or less in the position of representatives of the share-holding governments. The inclusion of a few non-officials in the boards does not necessarily have the healthy effect of providing a proper balance as between the philosophies of the government directors and those of the commercially minded individuals.

Professor Ramanadham, who has extensively studied public enterprises in India, observes that "the board composition is, by and large, such that there is a general tendency for the centrali-

---

[20] Daniel Spencer subdivides the control group in the public sector into a policy-interest and a managerial-interest group. The former is identified as the group formulating a generalized economic program. The policy decisions within this control group are arrived at in a complex fashion. Each department of the government has interests which are more often than not in conflict. Resolutions of important issues are determined on broad fronts. This process goes on at various echelons from the cabinet level down. High executives are not legal trustees, but are front men backstopped by departments and bureaus of staff personnel who beat out policy positions for their top men through much consultation and exchange. In India's case the institutionalization of this whole process is not obvious to the outside observer but there is some indication that the focal point for resolving conflicting interests and arriving at a policy decision is centered in the Planning Commission. See Daniel L. Spencer, *India, Mixed Enterprise and Western Business* (The Hague: Martinus Nijhoff, 1959), pp. 183-184.

zation of most decisional processes. The civil servants sitting on the boards are used to it and it appeals to them as a necessary legacy of a conglomeration of circumstances in which they presume to be carrying out, covertly or overtly, some departmental or ministerial policy."[21]

Another observation made by Professor V.K.R.V. Rao is that "there is no doubt that management both at the top level as well as middle levels forms the most important instrument for the development of the economy. The growth of public enterprises cannot be determined merely by resolutions or by centrally formulated rules and regulations..." A great deal has to be left to the discretion, intelligence, imagination, confidence and initiative of the persons who are in charge of decision-making in individual enterprises."[22]

One can go on and cite numerous observations relevant to the "decision-making process" in the public sector enterprises. One inevitable inference is that it is centralized. Centralized decision-making *per se* is not ominous. Even in some of the highly industrialized countries such as Japan, and Western European countries, decision-making is highly centralized. But the question that remains to be systematically asked is: Does a highly centralized decision-making process foster effective management of the enterprise or not? Is it effective, that is in terms of the defined goals and sub-goals for the enterprise?

There is the problem of reconciling managerial initiative and autonomy with ministerial accountability to Parliament. As V.K.R.V. Rao expressed, "We cannot let the bugbear of public accountability to operate so as to kill enthusiasm and initiative in individual enterprises and prevent them from growing to the levels of output and efficiency that they must rise to, if they are to play a significant role in the building of the Indian economy."[23] The question of how to resolve such conflicts may be approached by making the second inference, that is, the so-called decision-making process as one can observe in the public enterprises is nebulous. Policy-making and decision-making are construed as

[21] V. V. Ramanadham, *The Structure of Public Enterprise in India* (New York: Asia Publishing House, 1961) p. 182.
[22] V. K. R. V. Rao, "The Role of Public Enterprises in the Indian Economy," *Indian Journal of Public Administration*, Vol. 10, No. 3, July-Sept., 1964, p. 421.
[23] *Ibid.*

being synonymous. This is the general case in management literature. The public enterprises provide an excellent proving-
ground for a desirable distinction.

Policies and decisions are conceptually distinct. As Professor
J. W. Forrester recently put it, "Policies are those rules which
guide decisions. The policy treats the general case and at least
partially defines how specific decisions under that policy are to be
made. Conversely, a decision takes the status and information of
the system and processes it in accordance with the guiding policy
to determine current action."[24] By so viewing, attempts could be
made to delineate the policy-making function from the decision-
making function in the enterprise. Since India professes a social-
ist-pattern of society, one could expect that the broad guidelines
or policies for individual enterprises in the public sector would be
distilled from the general philosophy and would be more or less
similar in all enterprises within the public sector.

Again, as Professor Forrester stated, "In technology we expect
bold experiments that test ideas...but in matters of social organization we usually propose only timid modifications..."[25] Then,
for purposes of restructuring the decision-making process, that is
from the point of view of providing greater autonomy for the
enterprises than before, can an experiment, not a simulated one,
be made in the public sector? These writers would say yes. Without
going into the details of how such an experiment could be designed,
one could substantiate it by saying (1) that such an experiment
could be quite consistent with the socio-economic experiments
that are carried on in the present day world, (2) that such an
experiment could provide a basis and a rationale to design corporate forms of organization which could live up to their potential
and play their role in economic development, and (3) that just as
a change to industrialization accompanied by centralized decision-making experimentation may suggest a reversal that is,
within the framework of the common policy, decision-making
perhaps can be returned to the individual person.

[24] Jay W. Forrester, "A New Corporate Design," *Industrial Management Review*
Volume 7, Number 1, Fall 1965, pp. 5-18.
[25] *Ibid.*

Summary

Technological elements are most amenable to transfer from one country to another. Managerial know-how (including organization know-how) is as important as engineering know-how. The chapter endeavored to examine the theories of goal-setting and decision-making in the Indian context at a theoretical level. Specifically these two issues were raised and examined in terms of the large complex public sector industrial enterprises in India.

Some of the essential features of the culture-bound management-organization theories were brought out to formulate a frame of reference. Among the several perspectives, the one which regards organization as a production system was chosen as the most applicable in the Indian context. It is within this frame of reference that goal-setting and decision-making theories were examined.

Two modes of theorizing goal-setting in enterprises were noted: economic and behavioral. Profit as the goal for the enterprise was regarded as consistent with the societal goal in India. It was posited that the two sets of theories can be incorporated into one approach to study goal-setting in public enterprises. The approach suggested was that profit as the enterprise goal set through the process of learning and bargaining would define various criteria for reaching enterprise goals and lead to fulfillment of societal goals in India.

The theory of decision-making was construed as the theory of the process of decision-making. This decision-making process in the public sector enterprises was characterized as centralized and often nebulous. A distinction was made between policy-making and decision-making. The theory of decision-making process was found relevant to the Indian context and in order to determine the applicability of such a theory a real-life experiment in decision-making was suggested.

Prospects for Further Research

Organizational goals have long been a means of representing organizational character. They manifest what things are valued, what objectives the managerial, governmental, and other groups (in India) propose to pursue and the ways and means of achieving these objectives. Considerable attention is paid to the concept of goal and process of goal-setting in the public enterprises in India contemporarily. In the discourse of a textbook it is plausible to assume the existence of goals in neat compartments. In reality, goals are always surrounded by a thick, sticky coating of ambiguity. They are presented in various forms: aversions, concerns, interests, commitments, purposes, and regulations. Further systematic inquiry into goal setting may be in the direction of (1) minimizing the ambiguity with respect to the goals of the public enterprises; (2) formulating a hierarchy of goals (3) developing managerial philosophy in consonance with the goals. It is difficult to overstate the role that goals play in the process of an organization, because they are so crucial and fundamental. From the point of view of systematically studying organizations, that is public enterprises, the starting point ought to be the goals of these organizations.

The roots of decision-making process are deep in the subsoil of an organization. Hidden from commonsense observations they lie beneath the forms and rituals of organizations, and therefore the full character of decision-making process is seldom easily perceived. The suggested experiment which calls for bold action is likely to provide some fruitful data to perceive the decision-making process in a public enterprise in terms of ascertaining what the occasions for making decisions are, how exactly are the possible courses of actions taken, and how the choice among the courses of action takes place. These insights will have a considerable bearing upon the effectiveness of the enterprises in terms of the goals defined for them.

CHAPTER 5

APPLICABILITY OF AMERICAN MANAGEMENT*

The Indian Government as well as the business community has realized the importance of advanced management know-how in our economic and industrial efforts. The awareness and actions taken so far are reflected by several factors discussed in Chapter 3.

One of the paramount questions which remains to be empirically answered is: "Under what conditions, and to what extent, advanced management know-how developed and practiced in western countries, particularly in the United States, can and should be adapted in industrial enterprises in India?" In other words, as K. S. Basu, the Director of the J. B. Institute of Management Studies in Bombay pointed out, "The question will have to be faced and solved very soon as to whether the most modern techniques and practices of management evolved in more industrially advanced countries are universally applicable or should different management systems be evolved, developed and applied to different cultures?"[1]

The empirical evidence is thus far lacking in ascertaining the impact of culture and socio-economic, political and legal environmental factors on management practices and effectiveness. This is not to say, however, that nothing has been done in this area. On the contrary, much has been written on this subject, but to date there is no clear-cut answer to the problem of transferability of management know-how from one country to another (or from one culture to another). In this regard, management literature is surrounded by many controversies.

* The main ideas of this chapter were originally presented by A. R. Negandhi at the Academy of Management, Western 1965 meetings and subsequently published in *Academy of Management Journal*, Dec. 1965. Permission of the Journal is acknowledged.
[1] K. S. Basu, "Management Similarities and Differences Under Different Cultures," *Indian Management* (September 1965) p. 18.

Controversial Propositions

One "school of thought" asserts that "management is management where-ever practiced, a universal profession whose principles can be applied in every organized form of human activity."[2] As against this claim, many cross-cultural theorists like French and Israel, Harbison and Burgess, Hartmann, Kerr and Dunlop, Dill, Whyte, Gonzalez and McMillan, Oberg, and Farmer and Richman believe that the socio-economic, legal, political and cultural environmental forces affect and determine both management practices and effectiveness.[3]

For example, French and Israel, who replicated an experiment on "participation, decision-making and productivity" in a Norwegian firm, found that Norwegian workers did not consider participation as legitimate activity, as contrasted to American workers who viewed participation as legitimate activity; consequently, the effects of participation in Norway were significantly different than in the United States.

A study by Harbison and Burgess[4] also showed that European workers view participation differently than the American workers. Whyte[5] has confirmed this with regard to some countries in South America.

Gonzalez and McMillan, in their study of the applicability of American management philosophy (practice)[6] in Brazil, found

[2] This type of view is held by what is commonly known as the process school of thought. The specific quotation is taken from Harwood F. Merrill's "Listening Post," *Management News*, vol. 36, no. 1, January 1963.

[3] John R. P. French, J. Israel, *et al.*, "An Experiment on Participation in a Norwegian Factory," *Human Relations*, vol. 13, no. 1, pp. 1-19; F. Harbison and E. Burgess, "Modern Management in Western Europe," *American Journal of Sociology*, vol. 60, no. 1, July 1954; H. Hartman, *Authority and Organization in German Management* (Princeton University Press, 1959); C. Kerr, J. T. Dunlop, *et al.*, *Industrialism and Industrial Man* (Harvard University Press, 1960); W. R. Dill, "The Impact of Environment on Organizational Development," in S. Mailuk and E. Van Ness (eds.), *Readings in Administrative Behavior* (Prentice-Hall, Englewood Cliffs, New Jersey, 1961); W. F. Whyte, "Framework for the Analysis of Industrial Relations: Two Views," *Industrial and Labor Relations Review*, vol. 3, no. 3, April, 1950; Richard F. Gonzalez and Claude McMillan, Jr., "The Universality of American Management Philosophy," *Journal of the Acadamy of Management*, vol. 4, no. 1, April 1961, pp. 33-41; Winston Oberg, "Cross-Cultural Perspectives on Management Principles," *Journal of the Academy of Management*, vol. 6, no. 2, June 1963, pp. 129-143; and Richard Farmer and Barry Richman, "A Model for Research in Comparative Management," *California Management Review*, Winter 1964, pp. 55-68.

[4] Harbison and Burgess, *op. cit.*

[5] Whyte, *op. cit.*

[6] The concepts, like management philosophy, management theory, and management practices, have not been defined clearly by many authors in management

that the management philosophy is culture-bound and "American philosophy (practice) of management is not universally applicable."[7]

Winston Oberg, in his study of "Cross-Cultural Perspective on Management Principles," argues that if the ground rules under which the manager operates are different in different cultures and-or countries, then it would be quite fruitless to search for a common set of strategies of management. From his overseas experience and empirical research in Brazil and in the United States he concluded that

Cultural differences from one country to another are more significant than many writers (on management theory) now appear to recognize ... If management principles are to be truly universal ... they must face up to the challenge of other cultures and other business climates ... (universalist claim) is hardly warranted by either evidence or intuition at this stage in the development of management theory.[8]

Farmer and Richman, in their model for research in comparative management, stressed the importance of external environmental factors on the efficiency of the manager. They argued that

Most studies of management have taken place within a "black box" labeled management, without much concern for the external environment in which the firm may operate. As long as this external environment is about the same for all firms, the approach is valid; however, in cases where the environment differs significantly, ... as is the case between nations, present theory (of management) is inadequate to explain comparative differentials in efficiency.[9]

In contradistinction to these cross-cultural contentions, there is also evidence that certain elements of American management know-how are successfully applied in altogether different cultures and environments. For example, Gonzalez and McMillan who have argued that management philosophies (practices) are culture bound, readily admit that "American management is most highly respected abroad...and it has yielded great dividends for the host

literature. Gonzalez and McMillan, in this article, are using the concepts interchangeably. For such confusion in usage of these concepts, also see John F. Mee, *Management Thought in a Dynamic Economy* (New York: New York University Press, 1963), pp. 73-74, where the author is using management theory and management philosophy interchangeably. In this model, however, the concept of management philosophy is being defined differently from these author's definitions.

[7] Gonzalez and McMillan, *op. cit.*, p. 39.
[8] Oberg, *op. cit.*, pp. 141-142.
[9] Farmer and Richman, *op. cit.*, p. 56.

country.[10] Harbison and Myers in their study of management practices in eleven countries observed that the "organization building has its logic...which rests upon the development of management...and there is a general logic of management development which has applicability both to advanced and industrializing countries in the modern world."[11]

Various research studies of the National Planning Association of the United States[12] also suggest that many of the American companies operating abroad have been able to use sophisticated management know-how in underdeveloped countries, such as Argentina, India, Brazil, Pakistan.

Kannappan and Burgess, for example, commenting on the performance of American subsidiaries abroad stated that

These firms stand out in their orientation toward modern industry and dynamic internal management policies. They are generally rated high in technical competence, quality of product, and managerial skill and are regarded as farsighted in recruiting the best personnel, in providing the best salaries and working conditions, and in delegating authority.[13]

These case studies of the American companies abroad, as well as the authors' own experience in India, do confirm the following assertions:

American companies operating in foreign countries are more efficient than domestic companies, and the higher efficiency of the American company is not entirely due to their advanced technical know-how but due to their managerial know-how.

Domestic firms using similar "hardware" and technical know-how have been proved to be less efficient as compared to the American companies. The domestic company using the American managerial know-how is regarded as more efficient and "progressive" as compared to other domestic firms not using such know-how.

Thus, if there are differences among the firms operating in similar socio-economic, legal and cultural factors, then one could argue that all the environmental and cultural factors may not be influential in changing the internal process of management. In

[10] Gonzalez and McMillan, loc. cit.

[11] Harbison and Myers, op. cit., p. 117.

[12] Ibid., particularly, see a case study of Sears, Roebuck de Mexico, S.A., (New York: National Planning Association, May 1953).

[13] Subbiah Kannappan and Eugene W. Burgess, Aluminium Limited in India (New York: National Planning Association, 1961), p. 25.

other words, there is no evidence which suggests "all" or "nothing" to the problem of transferability of management know-how from one country to another or one culture to another culture. The empirical evidence thus far suggests that there are some socio-economic, political, legal and cultural factors which affect management process and effectiveness and there are some factors which do not have an effect. To determine the transferability of management know-how from one country to another, therefore, one needs to identify the crucial factors affecting management process. To do so, however, we need some conceptual schemes. As Dill has pointed out:

> Administrative science needs propositions about the way in which environmental factors constrain the structure of organization and the behavior of organizational participants. Until we can identify relevant environmental variables and can predict their impact on behavior we cannot know how findings about behavior in one situation must be modified if they are to serve as prescriptions for behavior in other situations where groups are subject to different environmental demands.[14]

The model presented in this chapter is one such conceptual scheme to ascertain the cultural and environmental factors which affect management process and effectiveness. The following analysis pertains first to the assumptions, variables and their elements and second to a systematic inquiry within the framework of the model.

THE MODEL

Basic Assumption

Managerial effectiveness* in a given industry with a given technical know-how is dependent upon the way in which the manager carries out his functions of planning, organizing, staffing, directing and controlling. The way in which the manager carries out these five functions is termed here as management process. The management process is dependent on both the external environmental factors and the management phi-

---

[14] W. R. Dill, "Environment as an Influence on Managerial Autonomy," in J. D. Thompson *et al.* (eds.) *Comparative Studies in Administration* (Pittsburg: University of Pittsburg Press, 1959), p. 131.

* For definition and explanation of this concept, please see p. 75.

losophy. Management philosophy as used in this model is nothing more than what is commonly known as managerial policy of the firm concerning consumers, stockholders, suppliers, distributors, employee unions, community, local, state and federal governments.

Important Variables

There are four key variables in this model: *management process, management effectiveness, management philosophy* and *environmental factors*.

To date, most of the "process school" theorists have recognized only two variables, management process and management effectiveness. In the main, they have studied the impact of management process upon managerial effectiveness. As Farmer and Richman have pointed out, "most studies of management have taken place within a "black box" labeled management, without much concern for the external environment in which the firm operates."[15]

As mentioned earlier, various cross-cultural theorists recently have recognized and emphasized the impact of culture and other external environmental factors on management process and effectiveness. However, they have not gone far enough to indicate the way in which these influential external environmental factors could be ascertained. Besides, these researchers have considered management philosophy as a "given," a product of the culture and environment. It is indeed true that management philosophy understood in a broader sense is a product of a given culture and environment. However, certain elements of management philosophy can and have been "imported" successfully. In this model, therefore, we are concerned only with those elements of managerial philosophy which could be transferred to a different culture and environment. Thus, our definition of management philosophy is very restrictive and deals specifically with the policies of the firm across the six key interfaces shown in Diagram 3.

Management philosophy used even in a very restrictive way seems to have considerable impact on management process and effectiveness. Chowdhry and Pal,[16] for example, in their study

---

[15] Farmer and Richman, *loc. cit.*
[16] Kamala Chowdhry and A. K. Pal, "Production Planning and Organization

of two textile mills in India, have shown the interrelationship between management philosophy, and management process and effectiveness. In this experiment they found that the company with a "quick profit" philosophy and changing manufacturing policy had low morale and efficiency as compared to another textile company having a "product-conscious" and "long-range profit" philosophy. Both textile mills were using more or less the same "hardware" and technical know-how. Their differential philosophy, however, had an impact on employee morale, productivity (a measure of managerial effectiveness in the model), and organization structure, delegation of authority, span of control, and communication patterns.

The findings of Chowdhry and Pal have also been confirmed by the American scholars. Ohmann, for example, in his case study of the British shipyards, found that the "quick profit" management philosophy had resulted in low employee morale and productivity.[17] Similarly, Nowotny argues that the "short-sighted" management philosophy has been responsible for the low morale and productivity of the European executives and workers.[18]

In spite of its importance, management philosophy as a variable affecting management practices and effectiveness has thus far escaped the attention of scholars and theorists. Moreover, in the literature, management philosophy and management process are regarded as the same thing and these concepts are used interchangeably by many writers.[19]

It may be pointed out here that the identification of management philosophy as a variable affecting management process and effectiveness is neither an attempt to add to the semantic jungle in management theory nor to carve out a distinct approach to management theory. As Harold Koontz[20] has pointed out, management theory suffers from "indigestion" and adding more academic jargon will hurt rather than help the cause of management theory.

Morale," reprinted in Albert H. Rubenstein and C. J. Haberstroh, *Some Theories of Organization* (The Dorsey Press, Inc., and Richard D. Irwin, Homewood, Illinois, 1960) pp. 185-196.

[17] Ohmann, O. A., "Search for a Managerial Philosophy" *Harvard Business Review*, September–October, 1957, p. 41.

[18] Otto H. Nowotny, "American vs. European Management Philosophy," *Harvard Business Review*, March–April 1964, p. 101.

[19] See footnote 6.

[20] Harold Koontz (ed.), *Toward a Unified Theory of Management* (New York: McGraw-Hill Book Co., 1964), especially pp. 1-17 and 235-265.

Following his advice and lead, we have made attempts to define all the concepts used in this model as clearly as possible. These various management concepts are defined through the study of their elements.

Definition of important variables through their elements

1. *Management Philosophy.* As mentioned earlier, management philosophy is, by and large, a product of culture and socio-economic, political and legal environments of the country. But certain elements of management philosophy are "man made" and can and have been imported from alien cultures. The model, therefore, deals with those elements of management philosophy which are less culture-bound but still have considerable impact on management process and effectiveness. For the purpose of this model, it is defined as the expressed and implied attitude or relationship of a firm with some of its external and internal agents, such as:

a. Consumer

   (that is, the company's attitude toward the consumer.
   irrespective of market situation for a given product;
   the question of whether the company regards consumer loyalty
   as important, or is it simply interested in quick profits?)

b. Company's involvement with the community:
   (1) Community welfare activities
   (2) Educational institutions

c. Company's relationship with local, state and federal governments

d. Company's attitude and relationship with unions and union leaders

e. Company's relationship with employees

f. Company's relationship with suppliers and distributors

2. *Management Process.* The management process is defined here as the way in which the manager carries out his functions of planning, organizing, directing, staffing, and controlling. The detailed description of the items which should be studied under each of these functions is as follows:*

---

   * This list of elements is reproduced from Richard N. Farmer and Barry M. Richman, *Comparative Management and Economic Progress.* Homewood, Illinois: Richard D. Irwin, 1965, pp. 20-21. By courtesy of the publisher.

Planning and Innovation:

Basic organizational objectives pursued and the form of their operational expression.

Types of plans utilized.

Time horizon of plans and planning.

Degree and extent to which enterprise operations are spelled out in plans (i.e., pre-programmed).

Flexibility of plans.

Methodologies, techniques and tools used in planning and decision-making.

Extent and effectiveness of employee participation in planning.

Managerial behavior in the planning process.

Degree and extent of information distortion in planning.

Degree and extent to which scientific method is effectively applied by enterprise personnel – both managers and non-managers – in dealing with causation and futurity problems. Nature, extent and rate of innovation and risk-taking in enterprise operations over a given period of time.

Ease or difficulty of introducing changes and innovations in enterprise operations.

Control:

Types of strategic performance and control standards used in different areas; e.g., production, marketing, finance, personnel.

Types of control techniques used.

Nature and structure of information feedback systems used for control purposes.

Timing and procedures for corrective action.

Degree of looseness or tightness of control over personnel.

Extent and nature of unintended effects resulting from the over-all control system employed.

Effectiveness of the control system in compelling events to conform to plans.

Organization:

Size of representative enterprise and its major sub-units.

Degree of centralization or decentralization of authority.

Degree of work specialization (division of labor).

Spans of control.

Basic departmentation and grouping of activities. Extent and uses of service departments.

Extent and uses of staff generalists and specialists.

Extent and uses of functional authority.

Extent and degree of organizational confusion and friction regarding authority and responsibility relationships.

Extent and uses of committee and group decision-making.

Nature, extent and uses of the informal organization.

Degree and extent to which the organization structure (i.e., the formal organization) is mechanical or flexible with regard to causing and-or adapting to changing conditions.

Staffing:

Methods used in recruiting personnel.

Criteria used in selecting and promoting personnel.

Techniques and criteria used in appraising personnel.

Nature and uses of job descriptions.

Levels of compensation.

Nature, extent and time absorbed in enterprise training programs and activities.

Extent of informal individual development.

Policies and procedures regarding the layoff and dismissal of personnel.

Ease or difficulty in dismissing personnel no longer required or desired.

Ease or difficulty of obtaining and maintaining personnel of all types with desired skills and abilities.

Direction, Leadership and Motivation:

Degree and extent of authoritarian vs. participative management. (This relates to autocrats vs. consultative direction.)

Techniques and methods used for motivating managerial personnel.

Techniques and methods used for motivating non-managerial personnel.

Supervisory techniques used.

Communication structure and techniques.

Degree and extent to which communication is ineffective among personnel of all types.

Ease or difficulty of motivating personnel to perform efficiently, and to improve their performance and abilities over time (irrespective of the types of incentives that may be utilized for this purpose).

Degree and extent of identification that exists between the interests and objectives of individuals, work groups, departments, and the enterprise as a whole.

Degree and extent of trust and cooperation or conflict and distrust among personnel of all types.

Degree and extent of frustration, absenteeism, and turnover among personnel.

Degree and extent of wasteful time and effort resulting from restrictive work practices, unproductive bargaining, conflicts, etc.

3. *Management Effectiveness.* The following elements or factors are suggested for ascertaining the degree of managerial effectiveness. It is admitted that this list of factors is not exhaustive; however, all the factors combined will give us an over-all idea of the effectiveness of the management.

a. Net and gross profits during the last five years.

b. The percentage increase in profits during the last five years (year by year).

c. Market share of the company in its main product line and percent increase or decrease in market share during the last five years.

d. The market price of a company's stock and percent increase or decrease in prices during the last five years.

e. The percentage increase in sales during the last five years.

f. Employee morale and turnover.

g. Employees' evaluation of the company and ranking of the companies under study by the employee of each firm.

h. Over-all evaluation of the company and ranking by the general public.

i. Evaluation of the company and ranking by the consumers.

Diagram 3

The Model*

a) *Management philosophy or policy*   *Elements*

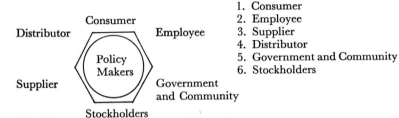

1. Consumer
2. Employee
3. Supplier
4. Distributor
5. Government and Community
6. Stockholders

b) *Management process*   *Elements*

1. Planning
2. Organizing
3. Staffing
4. Directing
5. Controlling

c) *Management effectiveness*   *Elements*

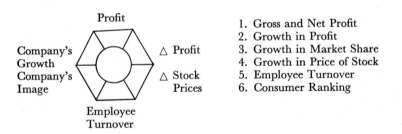

1. Gross and Net Profit
2. Growth in Profit
3. Growth in Market Share
4. Growth in Price of Stock
5. Employee Turnover
6. Consumer Ranking

* Based on the model presented here A.R. Negandhi and S.B. Prasad have been researching in various countries, and the preliminary findings will appear in their forthcoming book, *Comparative Management* (New York: Appleton-Century-Crofts, 1969).

Diagram 4

Experimental Design

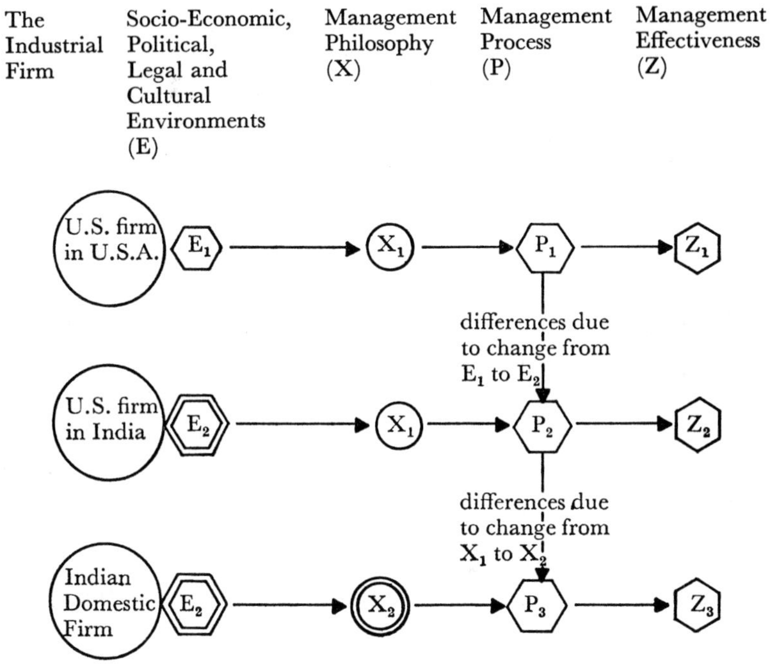

The Industrial Firm	Socio-Economic, Political, Legal and Cultural Environments (E)	Management Philosophy (X)	Management Process (P)	Management Effectiveness (Z)

U.S. firm in U.S.A. $\langle E_1 \rangle$ ⟶ X_1 ⟶ $\langle P_1 \rangle$ ⟶ Z_1

differences due to change from E_1 to E_2

U.S. firm in India $\langle E_2 \rangle$ ⟶ X_1 ⟶ $\langle P_2 \rangle$ ⟶ Z_2

differences due to change from X_1 to X_2

Indian Domestic Firm $\langle E_2 \rangle$ ⟶ X_2 ⟶ $\langle P_3 \rangle$ ⟶ Z_3

SUGGESTED METHOD OF STUDY

The method of study outlined here is based on the basic assumptions of the model. Therefore, it may be fruitful to recall these assumptions:

1. Management effectiveness is dependent upon the way in which the manager carries out the process of planning, organizing, directing and controlling; and

2. Management process itself is dependent on both the environmental and cultural factors and the management philosophy.

Thus, in order to ascertain the impact of environmental and cultural factors on management process, one also needs to determine the impact of management philosophy on management process.

Theoretically, one way of doing this is to emulate the classical Latin Square experimental design which permits the ascertainment of the effects of the experimental variable alone. To facilitate exposition, this method is expressed in diagram 4.

The problem is to explain the differences between processes P_1 (American company in the U.S.) and P_3 (Indian company in India). It is argued in the model that the differences between P_1 and P_3 are due to the differences in environments, E_1 and E_2 and in management philosophy, X_1 and X_2. To segregate the impact of management philosophy and environmental factors on management process, we need a situation where both management philosophy and environmental factors can become experimental variables separately. This can be achieved if we study an American subsidiary in India pursuing more or less the same management philosophy as the parent company in the U.S. In such a case, we can explain differences between

P_1 and P_3	Due to the environmental factors (E_1 to E_2 since these are different in the U.S. and India.
as follows:	The management philosophy is the same here and is therefore a
P_1 to P_2	constant variable, and environment is an experimental variable.

DIFFERENCES IN MANAGEMENT PROCESS

P_1 to P_3	Due to the management philosophy (X_1 to X_2) since this was different for the American subsidiary and Indian company
P_2 to P_3	in India. The Indian environments facing both of these companies were the same. Therefore environment is a constant variable and management philosophy is an experimental variable.

Now if we find that the American company in India is more effective than the Indian company (i.e., $Z_2 > Z_3$), then we can say that the management process (P_2) used by the American in India is "superior" to the one used by the Indian company, and an Indian company aspiring to achieve the same effectiveness as the American company in India should adopt process P_2. Though the process P_1 used by the American company in the U.S. may be still more effective, it cannot be adopted by the Indian company, since the environment in India and in the U.S. are not the same. It is possible that in due time the Indian environment may undergo changes and come closer to the U.S. environment. In this case, P_2 will be closer to P_1.

The Indian company desiring to change its process from P_3 to P_2 should, however, change its management philosophy from X_2 to X_1.

It may be recalled that this is just a theoretical rationale or argument. The author was not proposing that a study of only three companies could solve the complex problem of transferability of management know-how from one country to another, or from one culture to another culture. In fact, the author was presently undertaking a research based on this model in several countries, such as Turkey, Greece, Taiwan, India, Chile and the Philippines. The sample size of this study is also being greatly expanded.

Significance of Model

The model presented here will enable the ascertainment of the following:

1. The impact of specific external environmental factor(s) on the particular function(s) of the manager.

2. Provide an answer to our question of what elements of the American management know-how are transferable and what are nontransferable in differing culture and environment.

3. Identify the most efficient process in a given socio-economic, legal and political environment, and suggest the means through which this process can be implemented.

4. Identify the strategic environmental factors which do affect the management process and thereby managerial efficiency.

5. Determine external factors which are controllable and those which are noncontrollable.

6. Indicate the upper limit to which we could transfer American management know-how in underdeveloped areas.

Conclusion

India's economic and industrial development largely depends upon how well the society can organize and manage its human and material resources. Indeed, without effective organization and management, even a society endowed with rich resources can hardly feed and clothe its populace. But the society with proper organizational ability and managerial talents without adequate material resources can afford to provide decent standards of living. Japan is the shining example in this regard.

Fortunately, India is bestowed with vast, fertile land and rich mineral resources. But to fully utilize these resources in our scheme of economic and industrial development, we must develop and use effective organizational skill and managerial talents. Fortunately, however, we do not have to start from scratch. A vast amount of knowledge and experience of organization and management has already been accumulated by the industrially advanced countries. Indeed, the growing field of management and organization theories as expounded in the United States has numerous possibilities for theoretical and analytical efforts. Thus, we have to see that every effort is made to make the best use of the most advanced techniques and methods developed and used elsewhere. However, due to the different environmental and cultural factors in India, we cannot possibly adopt all the advanced managerial and organizational techniques and methods. It is indeed possible that what is developed and best for advanced countries may not altogether fit into our conditions. A heavy responsibility, therefore, rests on all those who are concerned with management research and teaching to develop a conceptual scheme to ascertain as to what advanced management practices and techniques can be adopted in the Indian conditions. The model presented here is only a humble effort of the authors to introduce some "scientific" thinking to solve the complex problem of transferability of management know-how. It is hoped, however, that the reader will treat this as just as beginning and accept the worthwhile challenge of developing new tools and methods to provide answers to such complex problems.

nterprise organized
by   s have aroused new
and   India operates in
a n   The pressures for
cha   d becoming con-
spic   than in the man-
ner   operations.

Th   e organizational
and   India. The dis-
cussi   anifold problems
confr   prises. The following analysis
is rest...cted to the problems of the new manufacturing and commercial enterprises and is focussed on four related major problems: (1) accountability to Parliament, (2) organizational efficiency and autonomy, (3) manpower problems, and (4) labor relations. It is desirable, at the risk of some repetition, to digress briefly on the context within which the public sector enterprises operate.

The Indian Environmental Influence

It is now part of the conventional wisdom that governments in underdeveloped countries, even those committed to a major extension of the government's management of the economy, account for only a small percentage of the national output as compared with developed countries such as the United States. Such a picture is somewhat misleading if one has in mind only the modern or organized sector of commerce or industry. A good proportion of investment in these sectors is now in the public

---

[1] Reforms in economic management have been put forward, and in some cases tried out on an experimental basis, in such Comecon countries as the U.S.S.R., and Czechoslovakia. Professor Evsei Liberman of the Kharkov University has been most articulate in the Soviet Union while Ota Sik has been the prominent spokesman for reforms in Czechoslovakia.

sector, and the latter's share has been growing.[2] Public sector investment in the First Plan was projected at Rs. 1,560 crores, in the Second and the Third Plan at Rs. 3,650 crores, and Rs. 6,750 crores, respectively. Another way to look at the enormous growth of the public sector is to examine the share of output. In 1950-51 public sector output amounted to less than 2 per cent of the manufacturing output in contrast to 25 per cent in 1965-66. For the same periods, the share in mineral output increased from 10 per cent to 33 per cent. These statistics illustrate the pattern of diversified and rapid growth of the public sector. However, the share of public sector in employment has increased much less rapidly and even today its share of wage-earning employment is by no means as striking as in some of the other developing countries. Also, for many categories of skills, particularly the higher administrative skills, the public sector is faced with a tight labor market, one which its own expansion could significantly affect.

The investment priorities in the public sector have made demands for new skills, especially various industrial and managerial skills, in projects which are not technologically different from comparable enterprises elsewhere. To some extent, it is true that the government in India has been a major employer of the nation's stock of skilled and technical manpower.[3]

The expansion and diversification of government activity have meant new and added strains. In order to appreciate these, one must recall that in many of the industries in which the government has new undertakings, the main burden of activity had formerly been carried out by private undertakings. Examples include the iron and steel industry, life insurance, shipping, and machine-tool industry. In many of these industries, except life insurance, airways and such, private enterprise has been allowed to continue and to expand. Industrial expansion has meant domestic and foreign as well as private and public industrial undertakings.

[2] See Nabagopal Das, *The Public Sector in India* (New York: Asia Publishing House, 1961), pp. 65-66, for comparable figures.
[3] For example, in 1960 the public sector enterprises employed 1.176 million professional and technical workers, 0.297 administrative, executive, and managerial workers in contrast to employment in the private sector in 1961 which comprised .299 million professional and technical workers, .097 million administrative, executive, and managerial workers, and 1.915 million other skilled categories. Source: *Fact Book on Manpower* (New Delhi: Institute of Applied Manpower Research, 1963), pp. 74-75.

The competition between the public and the private sector as a whole is not always free, notable being the absence of price competition, but in the area of competition for resources, particularly human resources, it is keen. Given the inelasticity of the supply of trained and experienced manpower, the government has had to draw upon its own administrative (civil service) personnel to man the new industrial ventures. The government's own stock of personnel and training avenues were inadequate and its ability to recruit the needed personnel depended very much upon its ability to institute innovations in its selection and salary policies.

Of particular relevance in this connection is the role of foreign private enterprises inasmuch as they are believed to practice liberal personnel and remuneration policies. Also, underlying the competitive state of affairs has been the general ideological issue of who could be the better employer, private or the public enterprise? The issues have posed a challenge for the public sector's capacity to innovate over such broad areas as labor relations, personnel administration, dynamism in the development of human resources, and organization structuring.

Investment choices in the public sector bearing upon the issues with which we are concerned is another important matter. The very scale of their operations have placed them squarely in the limelight and practically every issue concerning the public enterprises have been drawn into the realm of public controversy.[4]

In contrast to the private sector, many of the public sector enterprises are very large and these are also the enterprises which have attracted the greatest public attention. This environmental factor has undoubtedly affected the climate of operations of the individual enterprises, and particularly the issue concerning human resources as noted earlier.[5]

---

[4] The reasons for this are brought dramatically to the forefront when we consider that the capital expenditure for the Hindustan Steel Company alone amounted to $ 1 billion. This steel company is not the only one among "big" enterprises. "Bigness" *per se* tends to invite unfavorable public attention even in the United States. A detailed account of the nature and extent of the public sector can be found in V. V. Ramanadham, *The Structure of Public Enterprise in India* (New York: Asia Publishing House, 1961), pp. 1-52.

[5] *Ibid.* p. 3.

Accountability to Parliament

First, among the major questions raised by public enterprises, is the issue of accountability of the individual units to Parliament. The variety of forms which have been devised for legalistic purposes such as the company, the corporation, and the departmental enterprise, are of relatively secondary importance when compared to the organizational form employed and Parliament's (and the public) interest in assessing and influencing their conduct. The larger units have naturally commanded more attention and the discussions on state (as apposed to central) enterprises have been confined to regional forums. Unfortunately, a good deal less is known of the latter, although they are by no means insignificant.[6]

Given the scale of operations, it is incontestable that the elected popular representatives ought to be able to assess the effectiveness with which public funds are expended. Far more difficult, however, is the question of what forms this evaluation should take, and what the qualifications of the reviewers themselves ought to be. Underlying the first question is the need to spell out explicit criteria governing the performance of the individual units in the public sector. Where the criterion is one of profit maximization alone, the yardstick against which the managers of the enterprises could measure their performance is clear. Unfortunately such a simplified measure is by no means the governing one and as a result the Indian public enterprises, like their East European counterparts, have been beset with difficulties in specifying their maximum, and in some respects the criteria have become complex.

Some of the public enterprises have to fulfil certain goals even if their profitability is questionable. This may be justified either on the grounds of external economies or social policy. Examples are the mandates to the State Bank of India to undertake an unprecedented expansion of the number of branches, or the presumed mandate (as revealed during the Mundhra inquiry by former Justice Chagla) to the Life Insurance Corporation of India to stabilize the stock exchanges.

---

[6] *Ibid.* p. 21. A more general factual information on all of the major public enterprises is available in Om Prakash, *The Theory and Working of the State Corporations* (New York: Frederick A. Praeger, 1963).

It is also a general statement of policy that the public sector should aim at being a model employer. Public accolades to several of the corporations or companies in the public sector have further focussed on such indices as actual production relative to capacity production (for instance, in the case of steel plants), the record expansion (of Hindustan Machine Tools), success in opening up new markets (for instance, by the Air India International). Attention has also centered on progress in Indianizing the operational and designing phases, in the replacement of imported parts by domestically produced components, in achieving a greater inter-regional distribution of business, and so forth.

In general the more dissatisfaction there has been and the less clear the knowledge surrounding specific problems, the greater the alacrity with which generalized charges of corruption have been made. There have been some proven cases of corruption but in the absence of carefully considered evaluations the term has come to acquire ubiquitous currency leading to limited usefulness in developing criteria for distinguishing good from bad management. A major lacuna, common to all these approaches, is the failure to distinguish the opportunity costs of any particular goal in terms of efficiency as measured by the yardstick of profitability.

Crucial to the task of successfully insuring accountability to Parliament is the need to build a group of legislators with specialized competence in evaluating the performance of individual enterprises. The Estimates Committee of the Lok Sabha (Parliament) has attempted to play this role, but with limited success. The relative weakness of the legislature vis-à-vis the Executive has been a major factor, as the reports of the Estimates Committee, reveal cases of ignored recommendations. One should not infer that the recommendations of the Estimate Committee necessarily reflected sound business judgment. The ideological preconceptions which underlie the goals mentioned above and the neglect of their opportunity costs, at least partly, reflect the sentiment of Parliament. Competence in the exercise of legislative responsibility is not tantamount to formal academic training in economics or management or practical business experience.

In addition, the discontinuity in the membership of the committee precludes accumulation of learning and experience concerning the public sector enterprises. Thus, of the 30 members who made up the Estimates Committee during 1957-58, only 17 of them survived the following period (1958-59). The turnover from one session of the Lok Sabha to another is presumably even more. A point of contrast with the U.S. approach to similar problems seems relevant here. The various senate committees provide for greater continuity and seniority in their structure. Of equal importance is the limited provision of staff specialists to assist in the work of the Indian Parliamentary Committees. These issues of accountability to Parliament have an important bearing upon the organizational efficiency and autonomy of the individual enterprises.

Organizational Efficiency and Autonomy

Apart from formal and statutory restrictions on the conduct of individual enterprises, their autonomy has been circumscribed in other ways. Even where autonomy has been legally stipulated, the prevailing practice has been to designate senior officers of the Ministries concerned or officers who might be expected to abide by the wishes of the Ministry concerned – generally members of the Indian civil service – to form the top management group. The loyalties, career aspirations, and work traditions of these personnel have been far more closely associated with governmental departments rather than with the needs of industrial enterprises. Senior officials in the Ministry have thus been enabled, informally but powerfully, to set limits on the discretion of the individual enterprises.[7]

Functional control over the conduct of the individual enterprise has also been provided by means of "representing" the different ministries involved in the top management and by adopting routine control procedures (including accounting). The best known, and perhaps the most crippling, of this kind of governmental intervention arose from the designation of the Finance Ministry representatives to be on the top management of public enterprises. In some concerns, the Finance Ministry officers considered themselves to be less a part of the top management group

---

[7] In the Mundhra affair considerable confusion centered around whether a Finance Ministry opinion conveyed to the Life Insurance Corporation constituted a binding order or not. The corporation officials felt that it was but the Ministry of Finance denied this. See Ashok H. Desai, "Afterthoughts on the Mundhra Affair," *The Economic Weekly*, Special Number, July 1959, pp. 937-938.

and more a group of watchdogs with power, in effect, to veto decisions from being made or implemented. As Professor Appleby rightly remarked "the concern with precedent and routine review placed the most subordinate persons in the position of being superiors to the others in the highest levels of responsibility."[8]

In many cases, the scope for effective management in the individual enterprises has been narrowed down, and the enterprise managers have been precluded from introducing recruitment schemes, incentive programs, labor relations practices, and other managerial techniques.[9] Also, the enterprise functions of procuring material and human resources have been circumscribed. Consider, for example, recruitment through the Public Service Commission, or restricting the purchasing function by requiring detailed pre-expenditure and post-expenditure audit.

The restrictive practices imposed upon the enterprise by the Ministry, the Reserve Bank, or by the office of the Iron and Steel Controller, have also led to certain unfortunate consequences in the area of manpower utilization including labor relations.

Obstacles to Effective Manpower Utilization

Selection and salary practices within the governmental departments have not been very effective to recruit technical and managerial personnel. These practices have not only proceeded under a ceiling of income dictated by countrywide egalitarian pressures for levelling off incomes but also within the framework of civil service hierarchies. There has been a tendency among the public sector enterprises to emulate these practices and as a consequence many problems have arisen.

The salary structure for technical and managerial personnel in the individual public sector enterprises was hardly commensurate with that of private firms. Whether for this reason, or because of a reluctance to place independent men in charge, the top management positions in the public sector enterprises have been generally assigned to professional civil service personnel drawn from govern-

[8] Paul H. Appleby, *Re-examination of India's Administrative System with special reference to Administration of Government's Industrial and Commercial Enterprises* (New Delhi: Government of India. 1956), p. 19.

[9] The situation has been somewhat similar in other countries with the same civil ervice tradition. For example, see Louis J. Walinsky, *Economic Development of Burma, 1957-1960* (New York: The Twentieth Century Fund, 1962), especially p. 451 and footnote.

ment departments. Generally speaking, these persons continued to hold their tenure in the civil service from which they were drawn. Also their promotions, job conditions, fringe benefits, etc., were determined by the parent services. A major prerequisite for enterprise success was thus sacrificed; that is to say, the steward-ship of an enterprise should be in the hands of persons whose com-mitment to the firm's interest was beyond question.[10]

The top salaries naturally set limits on the remunerations which could be offered to other management positions, and powerfully influenced the managerial structure of the enterprise. Inevitably, the skills and attributes which gained dominance and relative importance within the enterprise deviated considerably from the scale of values which might be expected to prevail on purely functional and rational considerations. Thus, recruitment, se-lection, and placement in the public sector enterprises were con-ditioned by these constraints.[11]

Perhaps a good illustration of this point is the case of the In-dustrial Management Pool. The scheme initiated in 1957 had as its objective developing a reservoir of competent executives in general management, finance-accounts, sales, procurement, per-sonnel management, and welfare administration.[12] Seven salary grades with step increase in each grade (except the top two) re-presented the salary structure. The salaries for the top two grades were less than the salaries of top personnel in the Indian Ad-ministrative Service, and much less than those in the Indian Civil Service. Whatever the intent of the planned discrepancy, the result was that the Industrial Management Pool could effectively recruit only at grade levels III and below. This was quite un-satisfactory since, during the years after independence, the salary

[10] Furthermore, transfers, especially at the top level, from one enterprise to another, or from enterprise to government, impeded the development of commitment to one enterprise. In many cases, the top officials continued to exercise their senior govern-mental (secretarial) responsibilities. Although the reliance on administrative personnel has been condemned by the Estimates Committee, it recommended that industrial officers should be transferred periodically. See the *Nineteenth Report of the Estimates Committee*, 1958, pp. 42-45.

[11] There were a few exceptions as in the case of the Hindustan Steel where top men from private steel companies were hired. But these exceptions were minor and the limitations of the general practice were evident even when special recruitment to the management cadres was resorted to in the public sector enterprises.

[12] For an excellent review of these facts see H. K. Paranjape, *The Industrial Manage-ment Pool: An Administrative Experiment* (New Delhi: The Indian Institute of Public Administration, 1962).

position of even the high paid public services suffered by contrast with the private sector salaries.[13]

Was there an effective recruitment to the Industrial Management Pool, in fact? The results of the countrywide recruitment campaign do not attest to the success. The campaign sought candidates from the central and state government departments, from the existing public undertakings, and even from the private firms. A special recruitment board headed by the Chairman of the Union Public Service Commission did the selection. Among the 15,000 applicants, job offers were made to 207 candidates. No one was offered grade I, and only 13 people were offered grades II and III. Overall, there were 138 candidates and 131 of them finally joined the Pool. Among the 131 only 8 persons had previous technical experience. Since this mass recruitment was done by a separate board without reference to the personnel needs of the individual enterprises there was a considerable problem in placing the selected candidates. A majority of these ill-planned placements was in positions of a general character.

Very few specialists, either technological or managerial, had been successfully recruited, and the overall recruitment fell far below the initial target of 200 managers for the pool. The scheme has rightly been termed a failure.

Inadequate and rigid recruitment policies are but one aspect of the task of effective manpower utilization. There must also be adequate avenues for placement, for training and development, for appraisal of work performed, and finally for promotion.

Since no firm or enterprise is an isolated unit in the economy concurrently there should also be flexibility in internal wage administration to correspond to the realities of the supply of and the demand for various skills in the economy. The performance of the public sector has been notably sluggish in these respects, leading to what some observers have called a "flight" of technical personnel from public enterprises.

An authoritative study has summed up the situation as serious though not alarming.[14] The author has warned against the

---

[13] Government of India, Report of the Commission of Enquiry on Emoluments and Conditions of Service of Central Government Employees, 1957-1959, pp. 81-84.

[14] H. K. Paranjape, The Flight of Technical Personnel in Public Undertakings (New Delhi: The Indian Institute of Public Administration, 1964).

complacency to which the Government is prone simply because it is the largest employer of technical personnel.

Unless active and rigorous steps are taken to improve the public sector performance in respect to the many facets of high-level manpower utilization, the public sector enterprises may very well lose the hard-to-come-by people to the private firms or even to foreign countries. Continuous attention to morale, improved internal communication, and good human relations are all equally important not only to augment managerial performance but also to maintain a viable management team.

Labor Relations

To what extent have the public sector enterprises been the "model" employers? Indications are that they have not fulfilled this mandate with great success.[15] The first and the foremost reason for this state of affairs is the absence of sound managerial leadership among the public sector enterprises. Let us briefly examine how this has had detrimental effects on labor relations.

There are few, if any, of the major public enterprises which may be said to be excellent employers comparable to the best private firms. Although the public enterprises are subject to some of the same general regulations applicable to private firms such as labor legislation, wage board awards, compulsory adjudication and the like, their position has been more complicated due to the weakness in managerial leadership. A few examples from field interviews conducted by S. Kannappan in 1962 illustrate this weakness and its consequence.

In one case, a work stoppage was averted by an *ad hoc* settlement negotiated by the management but it was subsequently repudiated by the finance department of the same enterprise. In another case, a worker was hired at a rate above the starting wage for his grade and an interim appointment order was given to that effect. However, later on, when he received his wages he found out that he was placed at the starting level. Since protest was of no avail, the issue was taken to the industrial tribunal by the union, and finally a favorable award was obtained with retroactive effect. A manage-

---

[15] For appraisals, see S. D. Punekar, "Labor Unrest in the Public Sector," *Economic Weekly*, August 3, 1957, pp. 1015-1017, and Amulya Chakraborty, "Industry and Labour in the Public Sector," *United Asia*, vol. 12, No. 2, 1960, pp. 217-219.

ment order incorporating this decision was sent to this worker only to be followed by another order which terminated his employment.[16]

Although such cases as these may not be too common, the fact remains that a weak or poorly integrated management is not in a position to exercise leadership or authority in industrial relations.

Although there are capable individual managers in the public sector, weakness at the top level including lack of sufficient industrial management experience has precluded the development of the "personnel function." The manifold aspects of the personnel management function, in the modern sense, are unrecognized and unknown to some of the managers performing the personnel function.[17]

Far more important than the lack of prior experience or training, in a given management area, is the limited incentive on the part of top level management to cultivate competence among functional managers in the enterprise. Although senior public sector managers have been criticized for being lethargic in this respect, it should be noted that many of them feel only a limited sense of responsibility due to the manner in which outside intervention takes place. In the words of one informed person, "There is a general feeling among the top officials that they are being treated like dispatch clerks or like boys to carry out certain orders from Delhi and not as people put in charge of things." Thus the ability of the public sector enterprises to grow into "model" employers is weakened by this sense of lack of recognition and responsibility even at the top levels.

External pressures and informal communications may further strengthen such a feeling among top level enterprise managers. Some illustrative cases are (1) a top manager was first asked to favor a particular union leadership, and when labor disharmony developed, he was held responsible for it; (2) a manager who wanted to make a showdown with an unruly union found that

---

[16] A similar point is made by Laxmi Narain, "Labour and Management in the Public Sector, in V. V. Ramanadham (ed.) *Pricing Labour and Efficiency in the Public Sector* (Hyderabad: Osmania University, 1962), p. 54.

[17] Some officials whom S. Kannappan interviewed had only the barest idea of what modern "personnel management" entailed, and in one case the officer was not even aware of the relevant jurisprudence and practice which were then being promoted on a nationwide basis by the Indian Labour Ministry.

the Prime Minister was independently negotiating with the Union leader in New Delhi; and (3) a resident director who wanted to introduce an incentive scheme was told that he could do nothing until he received sanction and encouragement from *above*.

A related issue is that of workers' complaints that the public sector approach to labor relations is authoritarian. Although this is not directly related to the issue of organizational autonomy, it illustrates a reluctance to separate governmental responsibility for the conduct of state enterprises from its overall role as the sovereign instrument of the public will. Bonus, paid annually with an implied relation to the profitability of enterprise, was initially denied on the ground that the public sector profits accrued to the workers as citizens. Even state governments and officials of the Labour Ministry have at times been critical of the public sector enterprises for exempting themselves from certain provisions of the Indian labor code.

The above points suggest that in some respects labor relations in the public sector are more complex than in the private sector. There is no doubt that the sheer size, prestige, and newness of the public sector enterprises increase the magnitude of the problem. The politically oriented labor unions seem determined to unionize the public enterprises and rivalries are acute for this reason. In some enterprises such as the railways or defense undertakings, the legacy of old problems lingers on and further complicates the efforts to bring about improvements.

Conclusion

A general survey of the four problem areas dealt with in this chapter certainly needs elaboration and detailed study. But the available evidence presented here strongly suggests that the organization of public enterprises in India has failed to give adequate recognition to the effective utilization of human resources, and hence to their productivity.

Improvement implies an expanded concept of enterprise autonomy, and vastly enhanced scope for decision-making at all levels. All other aspects are only secondary to this.

A great deal has been said about corruption but poor management often leads to an action where it would be difficult to determine when imcompetence ends and corruption begins. If corruption is a sin, a far more serious culpability rests on those who tolerate conditions which favor ineffective organization.

The much needed efficiency and effectiveness in public sector enterprises will not come forth unless there is a clearcut indication that such efficiency is desired and that the necessary "price" will be paid to obtain it. The "price" will consist of both monetary rewards and the sacrifice of practices which discount initiative, technical competence, and ambition of the people which are in consonance with the interests of the enterprise. Unless such an approach is actually implemented, expressions of the need for efficiency would remain pious hopes and empty verbiage.

The most obvious place to begin is in the placement of first class, full-time, professional management men in the top positions and in insuring their commitment to the individual enterprises. Such men should be given considerable freedom, authority, and latitude and subject to a system which rewards good but reprimands bad performance. In the long run this would depend upon the effectiveness of internal management practices in the individual enterprises; in the immediate future, however, the search must be for top men from whichever quarter they may come, on terms which will maximize their full-time identification with the fortunes of the enterprise.

However, it is unrealistic to advocate greater autonomy without also improving policy formulation and its appraisal. Otherwise delegation can easily degenerate into questionable *ad hoc* decisions. The association of businessmen on enterprise boards is no substitute for such improvement at the highest level—and further raises the important, but neglected, question of conflict of interests.[18] Thus an essential parallel requirement is to strengthen policy machinery in government and Parliament.

The key to successful development in these respects lies in empirical research on the public sector enterprises and dissemination of the findings. Some efforts in this direction are made by the Indian Institute of Public Administration but only scholarly field research can provide the basis for further breakthroughs to overcome the barriers of secrecy, non-accessibility, and ideological controversy obscuring the real nature of the problems.

[18] These points have been developed by Mr. A. Subbiah, Member of the Investment Committee of Life Insurance. See Om Prakash, *The Theory and Working of State Corporations*, p. 235.

PART TWO

RELATED ISSUES

CHAPTER 7

THE SMALL ENTREPRENEUR AND ECONOMIC DEVELOPMENT

A popular argument for extending the public sector and direct state action for economic development in many of the under-developed countries is that there is a shortage of private entre-preneurs. It is now increasingly recognized that many under-developed countries may be held back, not so much by a shortage of savings (and investment) but by a shortage of skills and know-ledge resulting in the limited capacity of their organizational framework to absorb capital in productive investment.

Until recently, the role of the entrepreneurship in India had not received more than a cursory treatment. National preoccu-pation with the socio-economic problems, and the persisting pre-deterministic philosophy of life allowed little scope for the study or appreciation of entrepreneurial talents and their contributions. The term "entrepreneurship" could be viewed as a composite or a conglomerate in the economic context of India. On the one hand, there is the old and well established business elite; on the other, there is the new emerging State as the entrepreneur. In addition, there are numerous small entrepreneurs who have a vital role to play in the economic development of the country in more than one way.

This chapter is concerned with the innovating small entre-preneur in India. An examination of the salient characteristics of the Indian entrepreneur as compared with his American counterpart is made. The chapter also assesses the prospects which may be in store for the Indian entrepreneur and his contribution to economic development in India. The foregoing analysis is essentially based upon the findings of three empirical studies,[1] in one of which D. Unwalla was involved. Data from the writer's supplementary research are also incorporated.

[1] These three studies are: (1) W. Lloyd Warner and James C. Abegglen, *Occu-pational Mobility in American Business and Industry* (University of Minnesota Press, 1955);

Some General Patterns

As in the United States, many a small firm in India is run by the entrepreneur-manager, but in a majority of cases the firms are owned and managed by family-managers.[2] What is the distinction? An entrepreneur-manager is one who undertakes risks, starts his business, handles economic uncertainties, innovates new products, and processes, and undertakes all facets of management by himself. In contrast, the family-manager is the eldest male member of the family and he manages an inherited business firm. The former type is becoming more conspicuous and appears to have a more important role than before. For instance, Pritam Singh finds this type of small businessman especially in urban sectors an important source of entrepreneurship.[3]

The advent of the entrepreneur-manager is a relatively recent phenomenon which is noticeable all over India. As in the United States, the peripheral suburbs of cities such as Bombay, Calcutta, Delhi, and Madras have their share of entrepreneurship. They have become the major breeding grounds for this type of entrepreneur. Yet, the Indian businessman, in general, continues to encounter the negative, sometimes hostile, attitude of the community and the government.[4] Recognizing the repercussions of these attitudes, the late Prime Minister Jawaharlal Nehru is reported to have reminded the entrepreneurs of their social responsibilities and informed the public of their value in the future development of the Indian economy.[5] Even in the United States,

(2) W. Lloyd Warner, Paul P. Van Riper, et al. *The American Federal Executive* (New Haven: Yale University Press, 1963); and (3) Orvis F. Collins, David G. Moore with Darab Unwalla, *The Enterprising Man* (East Lansing: Bureau of Business and Economic Research, Michigan State University, 1964). *The Enterprising Man* is a behavioral analysis, in depth, of entrepreneurs found in 110 small manufacturing firms in lower Michigan. The study is concerned with men who started their own business enterprises.

[2] S. D. Mehta, *The Indian Cotton Textile Industry* (Bombay: The Textile Association (India), 1953, p. 84.

[3] Pritam Singh, "Essays Concerning Some Types of Entrepreneurship in India," unpublished doctoral dissertation, The University of Michigan, 1963.

[4] Charles A. Myers, *Labor Problems in the Industrialization of India* (Cambridge, Mass.: Harvard University Press, 1958) p. 26.

[5] cf. Joseph E. Stepanek *Managers for Small Industry, An International Study* (Glencoe, Ill.: The Free Press, 1960). p. 6. "Recently India has produced some financial tycoons on the model of America's robber barons, and they have not yet been transformed by public relations experts into industrial statesmen. But I think," continues Helen Lamb, "the low esteem in which Indian business is held is much more deep seated. The goals and value system of business enterprise do not permeate Indian society, as for instance, they permeate our own U.S. community. Indian business has had to

in the past, the word entrepreneur-manager itself engendered negative traits such as manipulation, greed, and avarice in the minds of people. Such an image has fast faded in the United States, but in India it still persists. As Helen Lamb observed, "Business has the power of money, in India, as elsewhere; but it does not have the prestige and general acceptance accorded business in the West."[6]

The entrepreneur-manager in India draws upon his family for labor but seldom for board membership in his business. While inviting one's own family members to be on the board of directors is somewhat common to the U.S. small business, it is not so in the Indian case.

The problems of organization and management which confront the small Indian entrepreneur are much more acute and serious than the ones which confront the small American entrepreneur. Consider a hypothetical case of a small entrepreneur in India. He foresees a business opportunity such as making and selling plastic hair combs. He raises the needed capital from his own savings and loans from his friends. If his business venture succeeds, he will have to face a series of growth-problems such as the need for increased capital for expansion, the need to introduce modern production techniques, the need to incorporate modern management techniques, and so on. As far as capital is concerned, the prevailing credit system is not in his favor. Even if it were, the entrepreneur's own thinking in so far as obtaining additional credit from outside may be clouded. As far as effective management is concerned, the Indian entrepreneurs are limited by their own incapacity to recognize the virtues of effective management, albeit the men themselves are highly ingenious, meticulous, and have unusual energy and self-confidence. They stand in significant contrast to the American small entrepreneurs, many of whom exhibit a greater "coordinating" type of ability.

operate in a cultural milieu which traditionally holds an organic view of society somewhat like that of feudal Europe." See Helen Lamb, *Business Organization and Leadership in India Today* (Cambridge, Mass.: Massachusetts Institute of Technology, Center for International Studies, 1956), p. 10. These observations, although made a decade ago, still appear to be quite valid.

[6] Helen Lamb, *op. cit.*

The Small Entrepreneur in India

The tradition-bound society of India continues to accommodate a large number of businesses which are managed by members of the same family. In big cities almost invariably large firms are run by old native families. Opportunity for the skilled workers is limited to small scale industry.

The family-manager forges ahead in an aura of indifference to socio-economic conditions. In many a case, he is excessively contented with the prevailing size and operation of his business. He worries little about competition, because in many cases there is little competition. The rapidly expanding villages and cities provide a constant supply of consumers even though he offers them little or no choice of merchandise and services.

The small entrepreneurial behavior in rural areas appears to be somewhat different from that of the behavior in urban parts. The following observations are based upon two surveys conducted by the writer, one in a village about 110 miles away from Bombay, and the other in the city of Bombay. The size of the sample is very small, less than 14 entrepreneurs in both the surveys and thus while no definitive statements could be made regarding the behavior, some patterns could be noted.

From the rural survey (n = 12) the following findings emerged: 90 per cent of them employed less than 13 workers; all the 12 entrepreneurs and their fathers were born in the same village where they had their businesses; ten of them had inherited their businesses. They were all concerned with providing higher educational opportunities for their male children. This aspiration appeared to be the single most important motivating force in their private lives as well as their business lives.

Conclusion

Besides the social and economic differences in the respective environments, there are other striking contrasts which bear upon the Indian and the U.S. small entrepreneur. In India, the entrepreneurial activities are highly tempered by the active role of the central and the State governments. As noted earlier, the central government in India, as in many other developing countries, has emerged as the biggest entrepreneur.

Until now, the Indian small entrepreneur has not entered into direct competition with either the government or the Indian big business. The growing Indian economy could accommodate many an entrepreneur without exposing them to the pressures of the buyers' market.

The liaison between the government and the small business sector has already begun via such organizations as the Small Industries Extension Training, National and Local Productivity Councils, and Asian Productivity Organization. Indications are that within a short time these organizations have accomplished a great deal by helping the small entrepreneur acquire managerial and other skills as well as technical know-how necessary to effectively play his role.

Additional help could come from the large business organizations. A large firm with its resources could help a small firm in the development of its managerial practices and technology.

The role of the small entrepreneur in economic development is not yet fully recognized in India. People still consider an entrepreneur as a shrewd man with manipulative abilities. The present image falls short of motivating people to embark upon entrepreneurial activities. Many bright, educated, and honest men tend to shy away from entrepreneurial activities for this reason even when they see a very promising career. Until such a stigma is eradicated, the small entrepreneur sector will not grow, and will only continue to contribute below par.

Along with a good image, the small entrepreneur will need an ever increasing array of innovations, both managerial and technological, to make his enterprise viable. The prevailing sellers' market blurs the need for such innovations, for despite poor quality and poor design, many products easily find buyers. Perhaps this could very well be the ideal time for many entrepreneurs to introduce improvements.

In fine, entrepreneurship in India, as elsewhere, is a complex and a demanding role. The small entrepreneur's accomplishments could be modest. A sense of "productivity-consciousness" coupled with a strong desire to change and to improve could provide managerial leadership so badly needed in many segments of India.

CHAPTER 8

ECONOMIC DEVELOPMENT AND MANAGEMENT EDUCATION IN INDIA

The problem of economic development varies in relation to the stage of economic development in which a country finds itself at a given time. For example, there were countries which had attained a fairly high level of development but which suffered severely during the Second World War and their economies had to be reconstructed. Illustrations of such nations are Germany and Japan. The underdeveloped countries of Asia, Africa, and Latin America manifest development problems of a different character, and even among these countries there is considerable variation in the stage of development at which each country has been. Nevertheless there are certain common problems which are similar in nature but different in degree. One of these, which is slowly being recognized, is that of the "managerial input" in the economic development model.

The role of "management" in economic development would vary to some extent in different countries. In countries such as the United States or Great Britain, the role has to be contributory to *maintenance of the existing high standards of living*; in the newly independent and developing countries such as India or Ghana, the role of "management" takes multifarious forms. Managers have to locate the resources of the country, utilize them in a constrained atmosphere, and sometimes do so in a politically unstable environment. The challenge is greater and the difficulties are more serious in the case of managers in the developing countries. Added to these is the lack of such managers in almost all of the developing countries.

This chapter is concerned with "management education" in India. The purpose is to evaluate the state of the art. In doing so, the early management education is briefly traced, the current status is briefly sketched, and an appraisal is made. C. N. Vakil has been closely associated with the development of management education in India for over a decade, and, having observed management education in the United States and several other industrialized countries; he, therefore, is in a position to make some normative statements.

Some of the suggestions made in this chapter are based upon the urgency of their need. In the rapidly changing world of today it is not possible for the newly independent countries to wait for long before they can augment the living standards of their people. The need is urgent; procrastination would mean discontent and unrest. A country such as India, as most of us know, is beset with many problems. To simplify, there are two basic problems: one, population and the rate of its increase; two, productivity – agricultural and industrial – and its rate of increase. The solutions for both call for colossal tasks. In the latter area, we need an institutional framework within which it would be possible, as a starting point, to generate a devoted band of managerial manpower in adequate numbers.

Management Education in India

The importance of education for management was not easily understood in India until recently. Even now many persons are not quite clear as to the utility and importance of management education, in spite of the fact that several activities have been organized in the country in recent years to spread management education. It may be appropriate to take stock of the nature of management education that has grown in the country to examine whether it is suitable for the requirements of the country and to suggest improvements.

The All India Council of Technical Education (Ministry of Education) took the initiative about 15 years ago and obtained expert guidance for management education. Since then the arrangements for management education have been within the purview of this body, although one may doubt the aptness of such an arrangement. It is obvious that the arrangements for such education have been colored by the outlook of the All India Council of Technical Education, whose main function is to develop technical education in the country. One of the first steps taken by this body was to encourage the inception of part-time or evening classes in management training in a few selected universities and technical institutions. By a curious reasoning due to the technical bias of this organization, they decided that courses in business management and industrial administration should be separated and should be entrusted to separate institutions. Accordingly, four universities were entrusted with the curriculum in business management and an equal number of technical institutions were entrusted with the curriculum in industrial administration. Commerce and liberal arts graduates were to be admitted to the former; science and technological graduates to the latter. It was not realized that these courses were essentially overlapping and that the difference was marginal. If these courses were organized jointly, it would have been possible to utilize the available resources more effectively, and bring together trainees from different types of industries and businesses which would have been an advantage in itself.[1]

It was necessary, however, to develop these courses in the light of experience and the growing requirements of the country. This does not seem to have been done so far except in Bombay, to which reference will be made later. The level at which these courses are carried out even now after many years of experience may be considered rather low. Besides formal university education there are other avenues to impart management education in India.

The Administrative Staff College at Hyderabad (State of Andhra Pradesh) is an institution for giving intensive management training to senior executives from the public and private sectors. A selected number of trainees undergo training over a period of about three months. By its nature, it is costly and it is available only to a small number. The time has come when it should be ascertained whether the intensive training given in this institution has been utilized in practice by the trainees, and if so, with what success.

There are several management associations now in the country with an All India Federal Organization on top. They organize occasionally short-term courses or seminars particularly when

---

[1] I remember that as a member of the Board in charge of Management Studies of the All India Council of Technical Education, I found myself in a minority of one in opposing such demarcation of management studies which was unnatural and uncalled for as well as wasteful. The realization came rather late to those concerned and this arrangement continued for some years. Later on the courses were handed over to the universities as in Bombay, although efforts have been made to maintain the distinction between them in practice *even now*.

foreign specialists are available. Some of these are useful, but some are rather exclusive. For example, a seminar has been organized for the last few years with the help of the Ford Foundation by the All India Management Association. The Ford Foundation invites American specialists in management for the course. It is open to a small number of selected senior executives from business firms. It is held in Kashmir during the summer for a few weeks. It is obviously exclusive in character because only those few who can afford the cost can participate. In this case also sufficient experience has been gained by now to ascertain whether the training imparted has been utilized and with what success.

Besides such efforts, the All India Productivity Council organizes management training classes for those concerned with small industries in different parts of the country. These are short-term courses and obviously very basic in nature. As this experiment is also going on for some time, it would be desirable to examine whether the practical utility of this training is established.

A few private business enterprises have their own training establishments for their staff. It may be expected that this would be properly directed to the desired end. While such training would be useful to the business houses concerned, it is obviously not available to others outside the organization and it does not therefore form part of the management training available to those who seek it. Among the business houses which organize such courses, we may mention the Tata Industries and the Hindustan Lever.

Other Stray Efforts

Besides this there are a few other efforts, rather of a haphazard nature, for management training. There are some organizations who organize short-term courses on select topics or hold seminars ranging from a day to a week and so on. These are widely advertised and carry fairly high fees. In spite of this, they seem to get participants which may indicate that there is a great demand for management training. While some of these are useful ventures there is a good element of adventurism in this effort. The primary objective of such organizations appears to make private gains out of the growing demand for management education. It would appear that not all such effort is of a genuine nature.

It would thus be obvious that although the demand for management education is growing with the rapid industrialization and economic development in the country, the supply of such trainees is not growing in proportion either in quality or in quantity. Some of the efforts are of a random nature; others are of an exclusive nature; some are intended to make profits and are not of the right type. It has so far not been the business of anybody to see whether the training is suited to our requirements and whether the training being given has been utilized, and above all whether there is any management literature adapted to Indian conditions.

University Type Education in Management

The curriculum in business management at the University of Bombay was organized by me as Director of the Graduate School of Economics and Sociology. It became a section of the Department of Economics. Not being satisfied with the curriculum, efforts were made to start a fulltime Management Institute somewhat on the lines of the Harvard School of Business Administration adapted to our conditions. A tentative scheme was drawn up by me to serve as the basis of discussion; this was widely circulated among those interested for comments. The University of Bombay accepted the idea in principle and had received a proposal from a business magnate in Bombay to give a large donation for the purpose of the Institute. The Ford Foundation was requested to take interest in it. They invited two experts, Professors Mariam and Thurlby, both of the Harvard School to advise the University of Bombay on further steps to be taken. I was asked by the University to help them in their work. They worked during January-February, 1957, and were put in touch with various business groups with whom they had frank discussions. They had opportunities to meet junior as well as senior managerial personnel in Bombay; they had also opportunities to meet big business as well as committees of the Bombay Millowners' Association, the Indian Merchants' chamber and so on. This had a great educative value inasmuch as management consciousness grew among those interested in it. They were in close touch with the work of the business management class in the University and with the trainees. They had also opportunities to discuss the tentative scheme for a fulltime course with appropriate persons in and outside the University.

They enjoyed meeting a group of about fifteen young men (M.B. A.'s) trained in American universities, who could discuss with them their experience of Indian conditions in the light of their American training.

Unfortunately the report of Professors Mariam and Thurlby was not followed up and for some time the idea was put in cold storage. My services were lent by the University of Bombay to UNESCO to work as Director of the UNESCO Research Centre for Southern Asia with head-quarters at Calcutta. I joined in March 1957 and could not take the necessary interest in the above report. The Ford Foundation was good enough to revive the idea some time later by inviting Professor George Robbins, Associate Dean of the School of Business Administration, University of California, Los Angeles, to review the situation. Professor Robbins was good enough to discuss his problem with me at the early stage of his work and also later when he had formed his tentative conclusions. The following is a summary of the recommendations made by Professor Robbins in his own words:

(1) An Institute of Enterprise Management should be established on an All-India basis. It must be regarded as a high-priority national asset, indispensable in the development of the resources of management, i.e., the manpower to translate natural resources, technology, and human talent into effective organizations to produce wealth. Accordingly, it must receive financial support from industry and government adequate for its needs in a planned, phased development.

(2) The Institute should be a post-graduate center of teaching and research where attention is focused on the most difficult problems of management rather than on the routines of business practice, and where education and training include the acquisition of knowledge, attitudes, and skills of management in business.

(3) The Institute should be located geographically (i) where there exist varied types and sizes of business to serve as a laboratory for the faculty and students, (ii) where adequate resources are available, and (iii) where the environment is favorable to vigorous growth and experimentation.

(4) The Institute should be inaugurated as an autonomous, independent organization with a broad but specific charter and

with a governing body representative of the highest ranks of business, government, and scholarship. The governing body should function to approve basic educational policy and budget, and to provide financial and other support.

(5) A permanent director should be chosen and assigned the responsibility of developing a regular full-time staff from which the detailed programs of teaching and research should emerge as recommendations to the governing body.

(6) A phased development should look toward (i) formal organization, selection of a director, and appointment of key staff members by mid-1960, (ii) inauguration of advanced or middle management training programs by January, 1961, and (iii) beginning of the two-year full-time course for post-graduates by the fall of 1961.

(7) A second Institute should be established as an urgent need as soon as support and staff are available, and its location should meet similar specifications.

Institutes of Management

It will be noticed that Professor Robbins recommended the creation of management institutes independent of the universities, although they were expected to work in cooperation with the universities. He found that the university atmosphere and regulations in India were not suited for the type of flexible arrangements that would be necessary for management institutes. He preferred therefore to follow the model of the Indian Institute of Technology at Kharagpur (W. Bengal), for management institutes that he suggested. The government, however, took time in coming to a decision on this report. It was felt that a beginning would be made with two management institutes of the type recommended by Professor Robbins, one in Bombay and the other in Calcutta. The Calcutta Institute was started in 1961. There was some delay in starting a similar institute in Bombay. The Union Minister of Education asked the Chief Minister of Maharashtra to undertake the work, and the latter negotiated with the donor referred to above for the donation. In the meantime, some other considerations, perhaps political, came into the picture and suddenly the decision to locate the institute in Ahmedabad instead of in Bombay was announced some time late in 1962.

It may be noted that the Calcutta Management Institute has the cooperation of the MIT School of Industrial Management and the Ahmedabad Institute has that of the Harvard School of Business Administration, although in the beginning it was understood that the Graduate School of Business Administration of the University of California, Los Angeles, was to cooperate with the Bombay Institute and later with the Ahmedabad Institute. The organization of these institutes may be described as below. The state government gives the land for the institute; the local industrialists raise funds for the buildings; the Ford Foundation invites American teachers from the cooperating American school and pays for them; it also pays for the training of the Indian staff in the U.S.A. The recurring cost is met by the government of India. A governing body representing the various interests is appointed. Both the institutes are in temporary rented buildings at present. Their own premises will be constructed in due course.

In the meantime, the Bombay University obtained a donation for a building for their management institute and have converted their evening classes into a full time Institute of Management, known as the Bajaj Institute of Management.

Some Further Thoughts on Management Education in India

This rapid review of the trend in management education shows that in India although the movement is in its early stages, the consciousness has grown and the concept of management education has been accepted. A good deal of systematic work will be necessary to put the present stray efforts in proper form, to weed out mushroom growth and to encourage genuine work. In this effort the impact of the two Institutes of Management at Calcutta and Ahmedabad will be of importance, though it may take some time to be felt. In any case, the movement has adopted American methods of training. In order to make it suitable for India, there is an effort to undertake research in Indian problems of management, including development of case studies. It is to be hoped that as a counterpart of rapid industrialization, we shall have increasing attention to management training of the right type so that the country can have a well-trained cadre of trained managerial personnel for its rapidly increasing requirements. In this effort, along with the available education facilities, two other important factors are the type of trainees and the attitude of employers.

The training given hitherto was mainly to those already employed in business and industrial houses. It is well known that the original recruitment of such persons may not always be on merit. In consequence, the persons who qualify for admission for such courses on the ground of being officers in business or industrial houses may not necessarily be persons of high calibre or have the requisite intellectual background. Whereas management training of such persons is useful, it precludes persons of merit from getting the training, if they do not have the necessary contact with business houses to be recruited in their employment. This defect will be removed by the new institutes which admit selected fresh graduates in any faculty, and give them intensive training of the type imparted in American universities for the M.B.A. degree.

Persons so trained will obviously be better recruits for a management career and will be available for employment both in the private and public sectors as trainee-managers. They would be in a position, after practical training on the job, to take up responsibility at the junior level. It may be desirable to arrange periodically further training for them, say once in three to four years. It should be also possible to utilize some of these persons in the future for the teaching staff of management institutions. If there is no favoritism in the selection of candidates for such training, and if they are admitted on merit only, we shall have a really efficient cadre of management personnel, who can be entrusted to fill the existing gap of trained managers in the country. These institutes have also special short-term courses for senior executives. It is to be hoped that the new institutes at Calcutta and Ahmedabad will set the pace for the right type of training in the subject.

Along with the development of management education on right lines, it is necessary that the employers themselves become management conscious and show willingness to give the best of opportunities to such trained personnel in preference to the type of persons they now recruit. If this is not done voluntarily, it should be possible for the government under the Regulation and Control of Industries Act to see that trained managerial personnel is utilized in a proper manner by industries in the country. It should be possible for a qualified person not only to gain access to industrial enterprise for employment, but also to reach the top, if he shows merit. In other words, there should be the elimination of the hereditary principle now in vogue in the assignment of responsible positions in some industries, so that it may be possible to make such positions available to trained persons who show merit and capacity. It is in the interest of efficiency of Indian industries and subsequently of economic development that this change should come as soon as possible. Besides, it is consistent with the socialistic pattern adopted by India, because it implies an equality of opportunity which is denied at present in many cases.

Such an arrangement holds good both in the private and public sectors. Just as in the private sector the hereditary principle should be eliminated in the appointment of persons to responsible jobs, similarly in the public sector the practice of appointing persons from the Civil Services or other services to responsible positions in public undertakings should also be eliminated.

Conclusion

It is hoped that management education will not be treated as a fashionable garb, but will be utilized effectively as a means of greater efficiency. Towards this end, we have to see on the one hand that the right type of management education is imparted in the country with due regard to quality, and on the other hand, the right type of persons are given such training, and that once trained, such persons are given appropriate opportunities to build up a career. It is only then that the best talent would be attracted to this career. For the same purpose, it is naturally desirable to change the outlook of the employing class both in the private and public undertakings; they should realize that it would be in the interests of efficiency that the existing practice be replaced by a more desirable practice of having trained personnel for responsible work in industries.

It is possible to find cases of employers who appear to be pro-gressive in outlook, take interest in management training or are associated with activities of management education, but who have not been able to introduce modern ideas of management in their own organizations. The traditional habit, the love of power, the want of trust in capable persons are perhaps among the causes, which explain this anomalous position. We may find in this very group persons who criticize loudly the deficiencies of the public sector, though they may not be taking adequate steps to put their own house in order in the private sector. It is to be hoped that such contradictions in our life, which are to be found in many spheres, are a passing phase of the transition period in our economic growth, and all those concerned will make efforts to adapt themselves to modern requirements in the interests of efficiency and national progress.

CHAPTER 9

PRIVATE FOREIGN INVESTMENT AND
ECONOMIC DEVELOPMENT

Like many of the developing countries, India's economic and industrial development heavily depends on the availability of foreign exchange and advanced technical and managerial know-how. Foreign aid from the various industrially advanced countries has thus far remained the main source in meeting these needs and fortunately India has received a huge amount of such aid from foreign countries. However, it is clearly realized by now that foreign aid alone is not enough to satisfy India's needs of foreign exchange and managerial and technical know-how. Particularly since the 1958 foreign exchange crisis, India's balance of payment position has been rapidly deteriorating. At the present time, her foreign exchange reserves are at the lowest ebb, and they might have slipped through the floor several times if the government had not borrowed some $200 million from the International Monetary Fund. Indeed, as the Finance Minister, Mr. Sachin Chaudhuri, pointed out in his recent budgetary speech, the shortages of food grains and foreign exchange are the two most important factors hindering India's economic and industrial development.[1] It is therefore imperative that the government do solve these two chronic problems.

One of the most important means to solving the problems of shortage of foreign exchange as well as managerial and technical know-how is to increase the inflow of private foreign investment.[2] Historically, countries like the United States and Canada were developed economically and industrially through private foreign investments. Also, the recent prosperity of Japan, Taiwan and Western European countries is to some extent due to the large in-flux of foreign private capital and enterprise into these economies.

[1] See Budget Speech of the Finance Minister, Sachindra Chaudhuri, reported in *Times of India* (Bombay), March 1, 1966, p. 1.
[2] Some of the findings of A. R. Negandhi originally reported in his *Foreign Private Investment Climate in India* (1966) and *Private Foreign Investment Climate in India (1965)* are incorporated, with publishers' courtesy, in this chapter.

However, in spite of our need and desire to augment the flow of foreign private investment, such investment has remained quite inadequate. To carry out the envisaged economic plans success- fully we need some $ 300 million investment a year from abroad, while the rate of investment from such sources has been approxi- mately $ 60 – $ 80 million a year. Moreover, the need of foreign private investment is likely to increase greatly in the Fourth and Five-Year Plans. For example, the preliminary figures released by the Government suggest that the total investments of the Fourth Plan will be $ 45.2 billion.

The large gap between the actual requirements and the present inflow of private foreign investment in India prompted an inquiry into the foreign investment climate in India – the favorable and unfavorable factors in the investment climate so as to pinpoint the various obstacles and impediments to private foreign investment, particularly the obstacles that are inherent in the Indian govern- ment's policies.

Three research steps were taken to collect the necessary data for the study: a questionnaire survey in the United States, personal interviews with top executives of American, British and Indian companies, and documentary research in the United States and India.

A questionnaire was sent out to 188 American companies either having investment in India or contemplating such investment. A total of 101 companies responded – response rate being 63.52 per cent. Some 82 executives of American, British and Indian companies were interviewed[3] in the United States and India. They were selected from different types of industries.

Both in the questionnaire survey and in the interviews, efforts were made to solicit the following information:

1. Specific factors influencing investment decisions of pro- spective foreign investors in India.
2. Foreign executives' evaluation of Indian socio-economic and political environments and specific policies affecting foreign investment decisions.
3. Market potential and profitability of foreign venture in India.

[3] The field research in India and in the United States was conducted during the period of October, 1963, through April, 1964, by A. R. Negandhi.

There is a dynamic milieu of factors which influence investment decisions of foreign investors in India. Therefore, it was necessary to decide which of these factors were more important and needed close investigation. To decide this, reliance was placed on two things: the previous research findings[4] in the area of international investment problems, and foreign executives' views on factors influencing their investment decisions in India.

In the main, most of the research studies disclosed that fear of war and expropriation and socio-economic and political instability were the chief obstacles to greater inflow of U.S. private investment into underdeveloped countries.

On the basis of these findings, it was decided to investigate such general factors as socio-economic and political conditions significant to foreign investors in India.

To decide what specific factors of policies needed investigation in order to evaluate Indian private foreign investment climate, executives of the American and British companies were asked about the factors which influence their investment decisions in India.

Findings of the Survey: In the Questionnaire Survey, executives of American companies in the U.S. (n = 100) were asked to cite five of the most important factors influencing their investment decisions in India. They listed 12 factors in the following order: (See page 116).

In the interview survey 54 executives of the American and British companies responded to questions concerning factors influential in making investment decisions. This sample included 22 American executives located in the U.S., 16 British and 16 American executives located in India. The interview responses concerning the factors influencing investment decisions are given below.

(See page 116).

---

[4] To encourage U.S. private investment abroad, particularly in underdeveloped countries, various governmental and private agencies have conducted studies to ascertain obstacles to such investments in those countries. These include the so-called Paley Report, *Resources for Freedom* (1952), Gordon Gray's *Report to the President on Foreign Economic Policies* (1950), The National Industrial Conference Board Study, *Obstacles to Direct Investment* (1951) the U.S. Department of Commerce Study, *Factors Limiting United States Investment Abroad* (1953), and various studies on international investment by the Stanford Research Institute.

TABLE 8

Rank order of factors influencing foreign investments: Questionnaire response

Rank	Factors	Number and Per Cent of Respondents
1	Future profitability of venture	80
2	Market potential of product	76
3	Indian foreign investment and industrial policy	71
4	Indian remittance policy	45
5	Indian foreign exchange policy	41
6	Taxation in India	37
7	Indian repatriation policy	36
8	Political situation	31
9	Social and economic environments	18
10	Availability of technical and administrative personnel	7
11	Indian labor laws	3
12	Availability of skilled labor	3
13	Miscellaneous	8

TABLE 9

Rank order of factors influencing foreign investment: personal interviews

Rank	Factors	Number	Per Cent
1	Indian industrial and foreign investment policies	30	55.5
2	Taxation in India	23	42.6
3	Market potential for our product	13	24.7
4	Political situation in India	12	22.2
5	Availability of raw material and capital goods	7	13.0
6	Various governmental controls	6	11.1
7	Availability of technical and administrative personnel	6	11.1
8	Fear of nationalization	5	9.3
9	Socio-economic conditions in India	2	3.7
10	Marketing facilities	1	1.9

On the basis of the findings of these two surveys, the following specific factors were chosen for detailed investigation:

Indian market potential.

Profitability of foreign venture in India.

Indian industrial policy.

Indian foreign private investment policy.

Indian remittance and repatriation policies.

Taxation in India.

Indian foreign exchange control and import policies.

These factors in the Indian investment climate are analyzed below. In this analysis, both the factual data and the evaluation of these data by executives will be presented. Also, to gain a better perspective of the Indian situation, international comparisons will be provided wherever possible.

Some Crucial Problems of the Indian Economy

The shortage of foreign exchange is perhaps the most important factor hindering Indian economic development. As the Council of Applied Economic Research stated, "Foreign exchange will be one of the crucial factors determining many facets of the growth of the Indian economy in the decade that we are passing through."[5] The deteriorating balance of payments position and drag on foreign exchange reserves are well known.

Another major obstacle to satisfactory economic development in India is the rising population. The 1961 Census gave Indian planners quite a shock. Instead of the 1.25 per cent per annum population growth on which the first two Five-Year plans were based, the Census revealed a 2.15 per cent rate of population growth during the decade of the 1950's.

In spite of heavy expenditures, India was able to maintain reasonable price stability until 1963. The consumer price index increased by 15 per cent in the 1958-1963 period, which, compared to many developing countries such as Argentina (91%) and Brazil (75%), was low.*

However, since 1963 due to the shortages of food, grains, and essential raw material and spare parts, the Indian price level has

[5] *Indian Economy: 1961-63 (Conditions and Prospects)* (New Delhi: National Council of Applied Economic Research, 1963), p. 96.

* See *Monthly Bulletin of Statistics of the United Nations* for data on Consumer Price Indices in Selected Countries.

moved upward. The consumer price index increased to 131 in
1964 and recorded a high of 172 in the first ten months (January
to October) of 1965. Similarly, the Indian currency, rupee, is
depreciating at a faster rate, and the recent devaluation of currency to the tune of about 36 per cent in gold terms reflects this
deteriorating situation.[6]

Views of respondents: Foreign executives, concerned with investment in India, also expressed their confidence in India's socio-
economic environment and progress. Of the 47 American and
British executives who expressed their views on this point, seventeen (31.5%) said that the Indian socio-economic environment
was very encouraging for their investment decisions; twenty-nine
(53.7 per cent) indicated that Indian conditions were satisfactory
for their investment, while only one did not think that socio-
economic progress was promising. It can be seen from the following table that the three foreign companies – Unilever, Imperial
Chemical Industries, and Metal Box, have earned higher profits
in India year after year than in their respective home countries.

TABLE 10

Net profits as a proportion of net worth:
Indian and parent companies compared for three major groups, 1956-1961

(Per Cent)

Year	Unilever		Imperial Chemical Industries		Metal Box	
	Home Country	India	Home Country	India	Home Country	India
1956	16.4	15.7	7.2	19.0	——	——
1957	12.7	14.7	8.1	9.2	——	——
1958	13.7	19.0	4.8	3.5	9.3	13.9
1959	15.2	29.7	8.9	10.1	10.5	16.0
1960	12.8	25.6	7.1	23.4	11.2	21.8
1961	——	——	——	——	8.3	18.3
Average	14.1	20.9	7.2	13.1	9.8	17.5

Source: Michael Kidron, "Behavior of Foreign Capital: Its Methods of Control in India," *The Economic Weekly*, Special Number, July 1964, p. 1265

[6] *Monthly Bulletin of Statistics*, (New York: United Nations, November, 1965), pp.
156-65.

The satisfactory profitability of Indian ventures also was confirmed in interviews conducted in the United States and India. Of the fifty-four executives interviewed, forty-four (81.4%) were satisfied with their rate of return on investment in India; two (3.7%) were not satisfied; while the remaining eight (14.9%) did not express their opinion on profitability.

Remittance and Repatriation Policies: Remittance of accrued earnings and original capital and increments thereto have been approved generally on a fairly free basis. India's record in permitting the remittance of profits and original capital abroad has been good, and the government has not placed any limitation on the amount of earnings from any industrial investment. In business circles these policies are termed highly satisfactory.

A large majority of the executives (86%) of the American and British companies interviewed both in the United States and India considered the repatriation and remittance policies quite liberal and reasonable.

Impediments to the private foreign investment in India

While the Indian Government has been able to achieve some success in improving the socio-economic and political climate in India, it has thus far failed to streamline its own policies affecting private foreign investment. Foreign as well as domestic executives surveyed and interviewed in the United States and India particularly made frequent mention of the taxation policy, the foreign investment policy, the foreign exchange and import policies, as well as the Government's apparatus for decision-making in these policy areas.

Taxation policy

The Indian taxation policy and its effects on investment – both domestic and foreign – have generated more heated discussions, publicity and research than any other Indian policy affecting private investment. The foreign investors in India considered this policy one of the most important factors influencing their investment decisions.

The taxation policy impinges upon the private foreign investor in three main forms:

Personal Taxation: Generally speaking, personal taxes are much higher in India compared to many developed and developing countries. For example, at the income level of 50,000 rupees per year (average income of foreign executives in India) the Indian income tax as a percentage of income is about forty-two to forty-five per cent compared to 23.0 per cent in the United Kingdom, 16.2 per cent in the United States, 15.8 per cent in Canada, 30.2 per cent in Japan, 29.8 per cent in Pakistan, 33.9 per cent in Burma, 29.2 per cent in Ceylon, 11.9 per cent in Malaya, and 5.6 per cent in Brazil.[7]

Taxes on Company Profits: The corporate tax rate on foreign branches of foreign companies is fixed at 70 per cent of earnings as compared with 49.0 per cent in Japan, 40 per cent in Australia, 53.75 per cent in the United Kingdom, 50 per cent in France, 51.5 per cent in Canada, 30.0 per cent in the Philippines, 40.0 per cent in Malaya, 37.0 per cent in Peru, and 40.0 per cent in Colombia.[8]

The corporate tax on Indian-based companies is between 56.0 and 67.0 per cent of earnings, depending upon the type of industry. This also compares very unfavorably with many countries. For example, the domestic based company pays about 49.0 per cent in Australia, 50.0 per cent in Japan, 40.0 per cent in Malaya, 40.0 per cent in Nigeria, 49.8 per cent in Pakistan, 46.8 per cent in the Philippines, 22.2 per cent in Egypt, and 36.0 per cent in Syria.[9]

Taxes on Intercorporate Dividends: In accordance with the budget proposals of February, 1964, all foreign companies in India will be taxed on their intercorporate dividends at a fixed rate of 25 per cent. This tax rate is, however, much higher as compared with many countries. Such countries as the United Kingdom, Australia, New Zealand, Canada, Ceylon, Malaya, Belgium, Norway, Finland, Greece and Japan do not impose this tax at all, while in the United States the effective tax on domestic intercorporate investment is only 7.8 per cent and in France it is 12.5 per cent when the investing company holds more than 20 per cent of the capital. Thus the high incidence of tax on intercorporate dividends places India in a very unfavorable position compared with other countries.

[7] *Foreign Investor and Tax Reforms,* (New Delhi: National Council of Applied Economic Research, 1964), p. 6.
[8] *Ibid.,* p. 28.
[9] *India: Business International Indian Roundtable, op. cit.,* p. 43.

Indian foreign investment policy

There is no single formal document that can be cited as the embodiment of the Indian private foreign investment policy. The Indian Government's attitude toward private investment is mainly reflected in the Industrial Policy Resolution of 1956 and various high-level pronouncements made from time to time. The industrial policy statement of 1948 set the early pattern for foreign private investment in India. In this statement it was said that foreign industrial know-how should be sought, but effective controls of new enterprise should be in Indian hands except in unusual cases calculated to serve the national interest.

The Indian Industrial Policy Resolution of 1956 prohibits establishment of majority-owned subsidiaries by foreign investors. However, in recent years this rule of minority participation has been disregarded. For example, English Electric Company, Consolidated Pneumatic Tools Company, Asahi Glass of Japan, W. W. Sprague of the United Kingdom, Parke Davis of the United States, Hoffman-LaRoche of Switserland, Italian Ceat Gomma, and Merck, Sharp and Dohme Company of the United States were allowed to own a majority in their Indian operations.[10]

Thus, there is little about Indian private foreign investment policy that is rigid. The Indian government is guided by pragmatism. The government does not wish to establish rigid approval patterns that cannot be changed should the times or the specific case so demand. It wishes to avoid any form of rigidity and to keep a flexible position so that it can say yes to a wholly foreign-owned venture if the "merits" of the case demand such approval.

However, this pragmatism in policy both helps the foreign investor and adds to his problem. He has no clear-cut answer as to what will be approved and what will not be approved by the Indian government.

A majority of the executives responding to the questionnaire survey and interview showed much concern about the flexible attitude of the Indian government in this regard. They considered this flexibility as a sign of the "ambivalent mind" of the Indian government. This can easily be seen from the following statements of Indian, British, and American executives.

[10] *Ibid.*, p. 18.

An Oxford-educated Indian executive said:

Changing our investment policy from time to time hurts us more and creates suspicion in the eyes of foreign investors. We should be very clear from the beginning about our policies.

An American executive said:

(Indian) policies may be fair but the government of India cannot make up its mind ... and frequent changes in the policies create uncertainties in our mind and do not give us confidence to expand or grow ... changing policies also create frustration.

A British executive in India said:

No general guidelines for what will be approved and what won't ... even Pakistan has general guidelines ... it is very frustrating for the foreign investor.

Foreign exchange and import policies

Under the Foreign Exchange Regulation Act of 1947, as amended to date, the central (federal) government and the Reserve Bank of India control and regulate transactions in foreign exchange and foreign securities in India, payments to persons in a foreign country, the export and import of currency and bullion or precious stones, and transfer of securities to non-residents. In practice, as far as importation of goods is concerned, the control is now chiefly in the hands of the chief controller of imports and exports. The import policy for each fiscal year is announced in the month of April by the Minister of Commerce and Industry. In general, the import policy is very restrictive, and the government is determined not to permit unnecessary drawings on the very limited foreign exchange reserves. As a result, both domestic and foreign investors in India find it very difficult to get an import license for even necessary spare parts and raw materials. However, the restrictive import policy has one clear advantage: it offers private investors – both domestic and foreign – a vast market, free from foreign competition. Many of the domestic and foreign firms in India are taking advantage of this situation.

As regards restrictive foreign exchange policy, the Indian government has indeed not much choice in this matter. The government, however, through its various export promotion plans, is striving to ease the foreign exchange restriction. But judging from the present situation, it is fair to say that this policy will remain quite restrictive for many years to come.

Government's apparatus of decision-making

Another obstacle to foreign private investment in India is the slow and cumbersome working of the Government control apparatus. The formidable array of forms to be executed and officials to be consulted greatly discourages both the domestic investor and the foreign investor or collaborator. One can easily visualize this difficulty of the foreign investor by merely looking at the procedural formalities. He must obtain:

a. An industrial license under the Industries Development and Regulation Act of 1951;

b. Approval from the capital goods and foreign agreements committees;

c. A consent for the issue of any capital stock under the Capital Issue Act of 1947;

d. A license to import capital equipment and machinery under the Imports and Exports Act of 1947;

e. An approval from the Reserve Bank under the Foreign Exchange Regulation Act of 1947;

f. A certificate of incorporation under the Indian Companies Act of 1956.

The net result of these excessive control measures is the creation of unnecessary red tape at all levels. And this irritates both the domestic and foreign investor. The latter, however, is more sensitive in that he always has the opportunity of going elsewhere to obtain quick approval for his investment.

A large majority of the foreign executives interviewed, approximately 87 per cent of the total, in the United States and India responding to a questionnaire survey in the United States mentioned that red tape and slow decisions on the part of Indian government officials were the main obstacles to investment in India. Their indictment of red tape and excessive controls can easily be seen from the following statements.

An American executive in the United States said:

They (Indian government officials) are as slow as molasses in January ... we are in many countries, and India tops them all in red tape and time consumption. You cannot move without innumerable trips to New Delhi.

An American executive in India said:

...bureaucratic red tape and delays are particularly irritating, to the point that in certain cases we have foregone opportunities rather than fight through the procedural battle.

Yet another American executive said:

Red tape has been fantastic ... we budget ten times the usual required executive time ... It is difficult to do business with the Indian Government at least insofar as starting a corporation is concerned. We find the Indian officials very hard working, very well informed and very gracious, but because so many are or seem to be involved in most decisions, a decision is difficult to obtain.

Red tape and excessive governmental bureaucracy also were considered the main problems faced by businessmen operating in India. For example, of the fifty-four United States and British executives interviewed in the United States and India, some forty-four executives (81.4 per cent) mentioned red tape as the main operational problem.

They also showed much concern about the conflicts that exist among different agencies of the Indian government, resulting in additional delays.

Some recommendations

Red Tape and Bureaucracy: It is true that in recent years government has made several attempts to introduce expeditious procedures. Two such attempts are the establishment of Indian Investment Centers in New Delhi with branch offices in New York and Dusseldorf; and the issuance of "letters of intent" to both the Indian as well as foreign partners within a month from the date of their applications. These measures will help alleviate some of the procedural problems faced by the foreign investor in India. However, there is still much more to be done in the direction of procedural reforms. For example, one of the most potent sources of delay is in the issue of import licenses. The procedure known as "screening for indigenous availability" is adopted for issue of an import license. This procedure requires applicants for import licenses to obtain a number of "refusal letters" from indigenous suppliers before they can be given the license. This procedure is very circuitous and time consuming, and it is doubtful whether the resultant saving in foreign exchange is worth the loss to the nation through delays in implementing new projects.

Another source of delay in obtaining foreign collaboration approval is in securing an industrial license, necessary under the Industries Development and Regulation Act of 1951. It is believed that the implementation of this act has created serious obstacles to industrial progress. For example, the Indian Engineering Association's research[11] suggests that the present system of industrial licensing control has led to indecision or to arbitrary decisions and has provided unnecessary scope for the misuse of power. To alleviate this problem the Association has suggested a change in the method of issuing the industrial license. Under the new system, the purpose of industrial licensing would be simply to register or record the intentions of the various parties proposing to set up new projects or to expand existing ones. The advantages of this procedure according to Engineering Associations are:

1. Industrial projects would be implemented more speedily through the elimination of a major source of procedural delay.

2. An industry would become more efficient through the removal of artificial restrictions on competition and through the establishment of units of an economic size, resulting in lower prices, improved quality and increased capacity to compete in export markets.

3. Unnecessary duplication of controls and multiplication of government decisions would be avoided, thus enabling both the administration and applicants for licenses to attend to other more important work.

4. The full potential demand of industry for raw materials, electric power, fuels, transport, etc., would be duly registered

[11] *See Report on Foreign Aid, Collaboration and Investment* (Calcutta: Indian Engineering Association, January 1964), pp. 7.-8

with the authorities concerned, thus enabling more realistic planning ahead for the vital sector of the economy.

5. Industrial licenses would cease to be a marketable commodity, and current speculation on trafficking in licenses would be eliminated.[12]

The Engineering Association's suggestions merit serious thought and consideration on the part of Indian planners.

Yet another source of delay in obtaining the Government's approval is the division of responsibility among various Government authorities for approving new projects. This involves the foreign businessman in several trips from one Ministry to another or between the Central and State governments. It is therefore desirable to concentrate the various discussions and decisions relating to each project at one particular point as far as possible. One possibility here would be to give a greater measure of responsibility to the State government to approve and promote industrial projects within their borders.

Private Foreign Investment Policy: As we have seen above, there is no single clear-cut policy which reflects the attitude of the Indian Government toward foreign private investment. So far, the government has been pragmatic in implementing this policy. However, the pragmatism itself has become an inhibiting factor and is looked upon by the foreign executives as a sign of "unbalanced mind" of the Indian government.

Indian planners, however, always have taken pride in being flexible in their policy measures. But if the flexibility creates suspicion and uncertainties in the minds of private investors, then indeed it is time for the Indian government to make up its mind about what they want. In particular, as pointed out by one of the foreign advisers to the Indian Investment Centre, there is an urgent need for general guidelines concerning what will and what will not be approved by the Indian government.

There is also a need to spell out clearly policies concerning the following:

1. Rules on equity
2. Royalty payments
3. Payment for such intangible assets as research and development

[12] *Ibid.,* p. 20.

Lack of Proper Estimates: It may be pointed out here also that in spite of detailed planning procedures and estimations, the Indian government has not found it necessary to arrive at some reasonable estimate of India's need of private foreign investment to carry out the envisaged plans. In the opinion of this author, the lack of a reasonable estimate is in part responsible for the excessive administrative delays and for not realizing the goal of increasing private foreign investments in India. The inadequate knowledge concerning the requirements of such capital may give an impression to those who are in charge of handling the problems of foreign investors that the work they are doing is not of paramount importance. Feelings of this nature are bound to slacken the work tempo of these personnel. Besides, a lack of estimate makes it very difficult to measure the degree of success of the governmental efforts in securing such investments.

Conclusion

Some Thoughts on Further Research. In the study of the Indian foreign private investment climate reported above, only some of the most important factors in the investment climate were investigated. However, the situation, such as investment climate, is indeed very dynamic in nature and so these "important factors" should not be regarded as constant. On the contrary, to be effective, one needs to investigate the investment climate on a continuous basis. Longitudinal studies are in order.

Secondly, this study was conducted with particular references to the foreign private investment with or without partnership with Indian companies. However in recent years, a new dimension has been added to the area of international collaborations. This is the partnership between the foreign investor and the host government. The potential of this type of collaboration in promoting economic and industrial development is indeed immense. To utilize fully this medium for economic development in India, we therefore need to investigate the problems and potential of this type of collaboration.

Study of the Impact of Foreign Collaboration on Other Domestic Firms: We know that the domestic company collaborating with a foreign firm has improved its managerial and technical performance for other domestic firms. However, the full impact of this has not been investigated thus far. The National Planning Association of the U.S.A. has done some useful work in this area, but its case studies of the U.S. business firms abroad are limited in scope.[13] More intensive case studies of domestic firms may prove worthwhile in increasing our knowledge in this area.

Study of the Role and Potential of Licensing Arrangements in Promoting Economic Development in India: It has been widely recognized that the licensing arrangement is the easiest medium for transferring technical and managerial know-how of the industrially advanced countries.[14] Besides providing needed know-how, this type of arrangement helps to overcome the problems of trade barriers, exchange controls, and shortages of dollars or other foreign currencies. However, the potential of this medium is not fully utilized. Many developing nations have some misgivings about the utility of such arrangements. This is manifested in their refusal to pay adequate royalties to foreign licensors. Study of the role and potential of licensing agreements and various impediments to such agreements may therefore prove useful in utilizing this medium in promoting economic and industrial development in India. (For a discussion of some collaboration issues, see Ch. 10.)

Study of Other Sources of Foreign Exchange and Managerial and Technical Know-How: The Indian government has thus far not tapped the other available sources to solve the problems of shortages of foreign exchange and management and technical know-how. One such source is the "rich" Indian living abroad, particularly in African countries. It is believed that the considerable number of Indians now living in Africa and in the United Kingdom have accumulated a large amount of wealth in gold, sterling

[13] See various case studies of U.S. business firms abroad by National Planning Association, U.S.A., particularly, *Study of Sears, Roebuck de Mexico, S.A.* (Washington, D.C.: National Planning Association, May, 1953).

[14] See Raymond F. Mikesell, "America's Economic Responsibility as a Great Power," *American Economic Review*, Vol. L (1960), pp. 258-70; Jack N. Behrman, "Promoting Free World Economic Development Through Direct Investment," *American Economic Review*, Supp. 1960, pp. 271-81. See also his "Foreign Licensing, Investment and U.S. Economic Policy," *The Patent, Trademark, and Copyright Journal of Research and Education*, IV (Summer, 1960), pp. 153-72, and "Licensing Abroad of American Held Patents, Trademarks, and Techniques," *Patent, Trademark and Copyright Journal*, Vol. I (1957), pp. 145-58. See also various issues of the same journal since the fall of 1959. See also C. McMillan, R. Gonzalez and L. Erickson, *International Enterprise in a Developing Economy* (East Lansing, Michigan: Bureau of Business and Economic Research, Michigan State University, 1964).

and dollars, and they are looking for investment opportunities in India. But thus far, serious governmental efforts in utilizing this source have been largely lacking. It is true that the majority of these rich Indians are traders, lacking the technical and managerial know-how necessary to run industrial enterprises. However, fortunately, there are a large and growing number of Indian scientists and engineers educated in the U.S., the United Kingdom, and West Germany now living in those countries. Thus a study investigating constructive ways and means for bringing these two groups together may prove useful in utilizing these sources in India's development scheme.

CHAPTER 10

FOREIGN COLLABORATIONS AND INDUSTRIAL DEVELOPMENT: PROBLEMS OF UTILIZING FOREIGN TECHNICIANS

Foreign collaborations which result in the transfer of technical and managerial assistance (and foreign capital) from advanced to developing countries, are a direct stimulus to economic growth. Conversely, the economic and political settings in the host country (and changes therein) have a direct impact on the contributions to be made by such collaborations. Some significant aspects of this interrelationship in the Indian context are examined in this chapter.[1]

India's efforts at economic growth have been called "the Indian experiment" because they are being conducted under democratic political institutions and under very difficult pressures, both internal and external. In contrast to China's Communist route, the Indian experiment is a test of whether traditionbound societies can change to dynamic modernity within the framework of democratic institutions. The success of the "Indian revolution" itself depends on satisfactory economic growth. But, uncertainty of economic development poses serious questions for India's political stability which is already threatened by problems inherent in the Indian development experiment (regionalism) and by externally imposed problems. The outcome is far from certain and the next few years are critical. The role of foreign collaborations – what it has been and what it needs to be – should be viewed within this context.

Foreign Collaborations and Industrial Development

In a foreign collaboration the foreign company provides the Indian company with industrial property right, services and capital. These provisions stimulate industrial development by encouraging the development of indigenous resources. This is the

---

[1] This chapter is based on A. Kapoor's doctoral dissertation, "Foreign Collaborations in India: Problems and Prospects" (University of North Carolina, 1966).

main idea behind foreign collaborations. For example, foreign collaborations give confidence to local investors and thereby encourage both the development of entrepreneurs and a domestic capital market. By providing technical knowledge, foreign collaborations greatly improve a country's ability to undertake domestic manufacturing. They facilitate a rapid rate of import substitution compared to what it would be under strictly indigenous efforts. Foreign collaborations add to a country's export potential by helping to establish new lines of domestic manufacturing. They offer the tools and concepts of management leading to a more effective utilization of resources.

The government's policy on foreign private investment has resulted in a new pattern of doing business in India, namely, the foreign collaboration.[2] At the end of the second quarter of 1965 (January-June), India had a total of 2247 foreign collaborations compared with a meagre 81 collaborations in 1957 (see Table 11). And although India still has considerable British investment, there is an increasing diversity of source (country) of foreign investor (see Tables 11 and 12). Five countries – U.K., U.S.A., West Germany, Japan and Switzerland – have over 100 collaborations each in India.

Table 13 provides a breakdown by industry of the foreign collaborations approved. This breakdown reflects the changing priorities of the government in terms of the industries to be developed and the interest of foreign companies in undertaking collaboration in them. Finally, it is estimated that at least 60% of all foreign collaborations in India are purely technical while the rest are financial.

India's Fourth Five-Year Plan calls for over-all private foreign investment of $ 1,72 billion or $ 3.5 million a year during 1966-71 – a rate that is four times the present rate, and most of the foreign investment must flow through foreign collaborations.

The objective in this chapter is to analyze the role of foreign technicians provided through foreign collaborations in facilitating the development of domestic industrial units. This role is, to a large

[2] Matthew J. Kust, *Foreign Enterprise in India: Laws and Policies* (Chapel Hill: University of North Carolina Press, 1964), p. 66. For a discussion of the effect of the Industrial Policy Resolution on foreign investment, see Anant R. Negandhi, *Private Foreign Investment Climate in India* (East Lansing: Michigan State University, 1965); see also Chapters 6-9 of the writer's dissertation.

measure, determined by the factors preventing effective utilization
of technicians and thus reducing the inflow of foreign rights and
services (and capital). This chapter specifies some areas of change
in business and government policies.

TABLE 11

Foreign collaborations in Indian industry: countrywise
(Cases Approved by the Government)

For selected years.

		1957	1959	1961	1962	1963	1964*	Totals**
1.	U.S.A.	6	10	77	57	67	55	337
2.	U.K.	17	52	126	79	70	76	574
3.	W. Germany	2	13	67	42	48	58	294
4.	E. Germany	–	1	4	5	10	19	44
5.	France	2	2	16	14	16	11	71
6.	Italy	4	4	13	11	6	5	56
7.	Japan	1	8	30	24	32	24	161
8.	Sweden	1	1	–	6	1	2	24
9.	Canada	–	–	3	6	–	2	13
10.	Pakistan	–	–	–	–	–	–	2
11.	Austria	–	1	5	4	2	4	19
12.	Czechoslovakia	–	–	5	1	5	1	18
13.	Holland	1	–	10	7	4	5	33
14.	Switzerland	–	1	19	19	19	17	90
15.	Belgium	–	2	2	4	3	5	20
16.	Yugoslavia	–	–	1	1	3	1	6
17.	Denmark	–	2	4	2	3	7	24
18.	Finland	–	–	1	1	–	–	4
19.	Panama	–	1	–	–	–	–	3
20.	Poland	–	–	6	–	3	3	13
21.	Hungary	–	–	2	2	–	2	7
22.	Others	47	52	12	13	6	5	202
	Totals	81	150	403	298	298	302	2,015

Source: "Foreign Collaborations: 1957-1964," *The Economic Times* (Bombay),
Nov. 30, 1964
* January–September
** For the entire period beginning 1957 and ending with September,
1964.

The following analysis is based upon personal interviews. (n =
104). Because of the type of issues explored, it was essential to
question the respondents in detail about their experiences with
the foreign technicians and the research and development (R &
D) secured through foreign collaborations. Therefore, direct

TABLE 12

Foreign collaborations with top ten countries

(Approved, January, 1957, June, 1965)

Country	Number of Collaborations
United Kingdom	642
United States	380
West Germany	327
Japan	179
Switzerland	103
France	76
Italy	62
East Germany	53
Holland	34
Sweden	31

Source: *The Economic Times* (Bombay), October 4, 1965.

interviews were used with the different parties to a foreign collaboration.

Initially random sampling was used for selecting Indian companies. The sample was limited to companies in Bombay, Calcutta and Delhi. During the early stages of fieldwork, a selected sample was developed because of the better quality of response and greater cooperation from selected companies. The selected sample was representative in terms of the licensors' country, products involved, year of approval and type of foreign collaboration.[3] A selected sample was also used for European[4] and American companies.

[3] The country of licenser of the Indian licensee indicates the following distribution; United States – 47%; United Kingdom – 15%; West Germany – 14%; centrally planned economies – 8%; others – 16%. The countries covered under "centrally planned economies" are the U.S.S.R., Poland, Yugoslavia, Czechoslovakia and Hungary. The countries under "others" are Italy, France, Denmark, Belgium, Sweden, Switzerland and Japan.

The foreign collaborations of companies interviewed cover a wide range of products: petroleum refining, plastic wire, pumps, textile machinery, metal industrial air control products, tabulators, vegetable oil mill, machine works, centrifuges, cement-making machinery, pharmaceuticals, drugs, fungicides, animal feed, plastics, synthetics, chemicals, metal foundry equipment, switchgear and motor starters, film cooling towers, portable belt conveyers and hand scrapers, distillery and brewery, food processing equipment, sulphuric acid and superphosphate plant, flour and feed milling, steel pipes, electricity and water meters, power cables, electric overhead cranes, steel alloy, paper manufacture, cinema cameras, cement pipes, ball bearings, tin and nickel plating, etc.

The companies interviewed indicate the following breakdown: before 1956 – 5%;

In arranging for interviews, particular emphasis was placed on selecting those government and company officials who were directly involved with foreign collaborations both in terms of project negotiations and policy formulation. Because of variations of views and interpretation of policies, the government officials selected represented different departments, ministries and levels of officials.[5] The officials of the companies interviewed also represented a wide range of positions.[6] The total number of interviews conducted with the various parties to a foreign collaboration are considered to be large enough to make the response representative. The following table provides both the numerical and percentage breakdown of interviews.

Role of Foreign Technicians: Findings

How frequently are the services of foreign technicians provided to the licensee? What are the areas and reasons for disagreement between Indian and foreign companies regarding the role of foreign technicians in Indian operations? Given the Government's definition of and incentives for foreign technicians, can Indian companies secure the type of foreign personnel they need? Where should Indians be trained: overseas, in India, or in both places? These are the main questions with which this study was concerned.

Data obtained in this study indicate that in nearly all "financial" collaborations and in most of the "technical" collaborations, the services of foreign technicians are sought by and provided to the Indian companies.

1957-1959 – 30%; 1960-1964 – 60%. The remaining 5% are mainly wholly owned foreign companies established before 1956. Foreign collaborations became the primary method of foreign investment after 1956.

The companies interviewed provide the following breakdown; technical-cum-financial – 66%; only technical – 14%; consultancy agreement – 6%; wholly foreign owned – 14%.

[4] The European interviews were conducted in London, Eindhoven (Holland), Amsterdam, Copenhagen, Oslo, Stockholm, Geneva, and Rome.

[5] The government officials interviewed were: deputy secretary, member of parliament, joint secretary, secretary, minister, economic adviser.

[6] *American companies:* staff assistant to the executive vice-president; director of manufacturing, Far Eastern division; assistant vice-president; vice-president international division; group vice-president international; manager, licensing administration, international division; treasurer, eastern division; director, project management; president, international division; vice-president, international, South-East, Asia; president. *European companies:* export manager; legal director; secretary; area representative; vice-president international. *Indian companies:* resident representative; chairman; plant superintendent; assistant manager; general manager; regional sales

TABLE 13

Number of foreign collaborations: industrywise
(Cases approved by the Government)
For selected years and selected industries

Industry	1957	1959	1961	1962	1963	1964*	Total**
1. Sugar	4	2	–	–	1	–	9
2. Cotton textiles	9	3	–	1	3	–	22
3. Silk & Woolens	–	5	3	1	–	–	12
4. Iron & Steel	2	1	–	–	5	28	37
5. Transport Equipment	4	11	6	9	14	9	77
6. Electrical Machinery, apparatus, appliances, etc.	11	12	73	44	54	37	314
7. Machinery other than transport & electrical	8	26	143		88	73	537
8. Aluminum	1	2	1	1	–	–	7
9. Basic industrial chemicals	5	4	3	3	4	11	32
10. Medicines & Pharmaceuticals	4	5	3	9	2	4	47
11. Other chemical products	6	14	29	18	11	12	120
12. Cement	3	4	1	–	4	–	18
13. Rubber & rubber manufactures	2	3	3	–	–	5	21
14. Paper and paper products	2	1	8	8	1	3	34
15. Others	9	38	129	123	108	120	681

Source: "Foreign Collaborations: 1957-1964," *The Economic Times* (Bombay)
   Nov. 30, 1964.
 * January–September 1964
 ** For the entire period 1957 through Sept. 1964.

TABLE 14

Interviews: number and percentage

	No.	%
Indian Company Officers	55	53
American Company Officers	18	17
European Company Officers	9	9
Government (India) Officials	17	16
Others	5	5
	104	100

Foreign technicians could be assigned to handle specific problems which arise in the Indian operations or they could execute
the over-all technical administration. The Indian companies
prefer to limit the technician's role to that of handling specific
problems and the stated reason is that these people are not familiar
with the conditions of operations in India but are more suited to
specific technical problems the nature of which would not be too
different from anywhere else. This specific role is also seen by the
Indian companies as a short-term role. Nearly 60 per cent of the
Indian respondents asserted that the foreign technicians' need
and importance diminish as operations develop and as suitable
Indian technicians emerge.

The role of the foreign technicians is seen in a different and a
contrasting light by the foreign collaborators. They tend to seek
general technical direction and control over the internal aspects,
particularly during the inititial stages. Their argument is that
Indian companies lack specific types of experience and the pace
of project development solely depends upon the concepts and
methods established and implemented during the initial stages.
The foreign companies also feel that the Indian companies over-
estimate their ability to take care of the new developments. They
also do not subscribe to the view of their Indian partners that the
importance of the foreign technician is only short-term; they
contend that the importance extends beyond the initial stages of
operations.

In addition to the differences of opinion concerning the role of
the foreign technicians, there seems to be a divergence of views
concerning the suitability of the foreign personnel. Many Indian
companies feel that less than the best qualified man is sent over
to India while their foreign collaborators contend that they do
make it a point to send the available best person. Although it is
said by half the Indian respondents that the foreign technicians
are "technically incompetent" there may be some truth in it
since the Indian companies may not themselves be capable of
evaluating the technical competence of the foreign technician.
Coupled with the allegation of "incompetence" there appears to
be a feeling among Indian companies that the foreign technician
does not divulge the technical know-how he is supposed to. This
feeling is more common among smaller and newly established

firms and is not echoed by well established large companies.

From these viewpoints which seem to be at variance it could be surmised that the nature of relationship between the Indian and the foreign company determines both the acceptance of the role of the foreign technician and satisfaction with his performance. In other words, if the relationship is harmonious, the foreign technician's role is perceived by the Indian companies as useful and services satisfactory. If the relationship is strained, then the foreign technician appears to be the most likely person to be blamed or accused for poor performance.

The role of the foreign technician in India is further structured by the Government of India.[7] To compensate for the high personal income taxes, the government has made provisions for tax incentives to the foreign technicians. Both the Indian companies, and their foreign collaborators consider the amount of incentives to be adequate.

Conclusion

There is no doubt that the foreign technicians, especially since 1957, have been playing an important role in India to the extent of fulfilling specific technical needs of the industrial enterprises, fostering technical and administrative activities among the Indian technicians and managers, despite the differences of opinions regarding their role as expressed by respondents in the study.

Data indicate that the Indian companies themselves have not made the best use of the foreign technicians. This lacuna may be ascribed to the fact that a large number of Indian firms do not trust their foreign partners in terms of their sincerety and interest in the Indian project. There seems to be a fairly strong feeling among Indian respondents that their foreign partners take advantage of their lack of knowledge particularly in the technical areas. The absence of an atmosphere of mutual trust and confidence is perhaps the main reason for dissatisfaction with the foreign technicians. This distrust appears to stem primarily from the "technological distance" between the Indian and the foreign

---

[7] For example, the Indian Income Tax Act (1961) defines a foreign technician as a person having specialized knowledge and experience in constructional or manufacturing operations ... or industrial or business management techniques who is employed in India in a capacity in which such specialized knowledge and experience are actually utilized.

partners. Of course, technical collaboration implies that one collaborator is technologically better equipped than his partners. Nevertheless, in many instances in India this gap goes unrecognized. In fact the gap can be reduced through increased managerial and technical development within the Indian enterprises.

Indian enterprises ought to give greater recognition to the role of modern dynamic management concepts, philosophies, policies, and practices. They should recognize that the over-all direction by a foreign technician could provide a faster and more efficient pace of development of *Indian operations through Indian personnel*.

Foreign collaborators, for their part, should continue to emphasize education and training of the Indian personnel and perhaps should take active part in launching company programs as well as encouraging business and academic associations to develop specific programs for managerial personnel.

The Government of India also has a responsibility in the area of foreign technicians. It should permit a longer duration of tax exemption than five years; and also should provide tax incentives to foreign trained Indian technicians and engineers to attract them back to India.

This study explored the nature of relationship between the two parties to collaboration. It would be particularly useful to study management relationships before and after a period of collaboration, and attempt to trace the process of communication and interaction between the Indian and the foreign personnel. Such an inquiry could provide some insight into the reasons for the changing relationship.

CHAPTER 11

HUMAN RESOURCE DEVELOPMENT FOR ECONOMIC GROWTH

Human resource development may be identified as the process through which a society augments the skills, education, and productive abilities of its people. In essence, it means increases in human capital. Human capital is accumulated and improved upon in several ways: through programs of education and formal training, training on the job, and through individual initiative. It is generally agreed that this process, if carefully designed and implemented, promotes economic growth in any country.

This chapter deals with the problem of economic development from the point of view of human resource development with reference to India. There are indeed legitimate and vital social goals of education – such as universal literacy and equal educational opportunities for boys and girls – just as there are legitimate manpower aims. Furthermore, these aims are not mutually exclusive. The primary concern of this chapter is with the manpower aims of human resource development.

It is assumed that a carefully conceived program of human resource development is indispensable for achieving the twin goals of social change and sustained economic growth. An effort is made first to synthesize current thinking and research in human resource development in general; second, in the light of manpower aims, an assessment is made of educational progress in India. Finally, those areas where intensive research endeavors could yield fruitful results for the education and training systems are indicated.

Current Thinking and Research

Whatever else economic growth might involve, the importance of the human factor in it can be ignored only at great peril. Man, in the ultimate analysis, is the measure and end of all progress. It follows then, that measures which improve his skills and motivations are at least as important as the ones which improve the tools with which he undertakes productive activities. Of course this realization is not new in economic thinking.[1]

In the present decade there has been a rediscovery of "human resource development" as an important issue facing planners in many a nation. Even in the serious discussions about economic growth interest has shifted from tangible to intangible factors. For example, Theodore Schultz has observed that "Measured by what labor contributes to output, the productive capacity of human beings is now vastly larger than all other forms of wealth taken together. Truly the most distinctive feature of our economic system has been the growth in human capital."[2] Simon Kuznet's thoughts are on parallel lines. "The major capital stock of an industrially advanced country is not its physical equipment; it is the body of knowledge amassed from tested findings and discoveries of empirical science, and the capacity and training of its population to use this knowledge effectively."[3] Such views as these are not confined to the academic thinking alone. They have also been shared by those directly responsible for national educational planning. For instance, the final resolution of a meeting of the Ministers of Education of seventeen Asian countries, in 1962, endorsed that "As an Asian intergovernmental meeting, we have seen for the first time that education is not only right for our peoples ... it is equally a factor which contributes directly to economic growth of our individual countries."[4] In essence, the traditional view of education as a highly desirable end in itself has been reinforced by the contemporary view that education is a means to economic development.

The vital role of investment in human capital as a spur to eco-

[1] The very first chapter in Adam Smith's *Wealth of Nations* dealt with "Division of Labor" where he referred to "the productive powers of labor," and "the skill, dexterity and judgment with which it is anywhere directed or applied." In the same vein Alfred Marshall as far back as 1898 remarked: "The older economists took too little account of the fact that human faculties are as important a means of production as any other kind of capital," in his *Principles of Economics*, p. 303.

[2] Theodore W. Schultz, "Investment in Human Capital," in *Readings Economic Development*, Theodore Morgan, *et al.* (eds.). (Belmont, Calif: Wadsworth Publishing Company, 1963), pp. 187 and 199.

[3] Simon Kuznets, "Toward a Theory of Economic Growth," in R. Lekachman (ed.), *National Policy for Economic Welfare at Home and Abroad* (New York: Doubleday, 1955), p. 39.

[4] United Nations, Economic Commission for Asia and the Far East, *Problems of Social Development Planning* (New York, 1964), p. 1.

nomic development has also been highlighted by quantitative analysis and some area studies.[5] Commenting on the experience of the United States, Theodore Schultz observed that the relative increase in human capital in relation to both conventional capital and income is the major explanation for the observed decline in the estimated capital-income ratio ... And, finally, that the considerable increase in the productivity and real income of labor is again a reflection of increased investment in education and training.[6] The findings of Schultz have been substantiated by a number of other studies, principally by those of the National Bureau of Economic Research.

Research in the area of human resource development has not been confined to the United States alone. Studies comparable to the American experience have followed in other countries such as Norway, Finland, Denmark, Sweden, Great Britain, Brazil, Argentina and notably, Japan.

What is the significant channel through which the process of education fosters economic growth?

The term "growth" has meant different things to different people (and countries). Whatever other dynamic elements growth might involve, its most outstanding characteristic is change in the mode of thinking and in the manner of doing things. Thus a condition of growth is a purposeful evolving of change, its institutionalization, and acceptance by the majority of people. It is in this sense that the process of education brings about further growth. Since change is conceived and implemented by man, his development thus emerges as a factor of singular importance to economic growth. It is reasonable to suppose that capital accumulation embodies technical change; however, since new techniques require new thinking and proper motivation, it appears fundamental that human resource development must accompany, if not actually precede, capital accumulation.

[5] For example, see K. L. Neff, *Education and the Development of Human Technology* (Washington, D.C.: Office of Education, 1962); John Vaizey, *The Economics of Education* (London: Faber and Faber, 1962); Theodore Schultz, *The Economic Value of Education* (New York: Columbia University Press, 1963); Stanley Labergott, *Manpower in Economic Growth* (New York: McGraw-Hill, 1964); Frederick Harbison and Charles Myers, *Manpower and Education: Country Studies in Economic Development* (New York: McGraw-Hill, 1965).

[6] Schultz, *op. cit.* pp. 188-192.

The prime movers of change in a country are enterprise managers, government administrators, educators, and others; in other words, the so-called high-level manpower. As the prominent manpower economists, Frederick Harbison and Charles Myers, suggest, "Since most countries seek rapid growth, the rate of accumulation of high-level manpower must be several times greater than that of labor or of national income."[7]

Education and human resource development should be viewed in the broad context of planning for economic development. That education is indeed one of the crucial factors for economic development is logical.[8] Proper education may unlock the door to technical knowledge, and open up new vistas in methods and techniques that were never dreamt of before, thus enabling a mass of people to become more useful and productive than before. If a radical change in the value systems and deeply entrenched institutions is a *sine qua non* for purposeful development, education then becomes indispensable.

Objectives of Human Resource Development

The manpower or human resource development approach to the planning of education and training in developing countries is primarily concerned with setting and providing for employment targets requiring the acquisition of skills in the modern urban sector. As Richard Blandy has pointed out, "For various reasons – such as the inadequacy of statistical data, attempts to include social requirements for certain kinds of manpower, concentration of attention on the formal educational system, and the neglect of the possibilities of improving the flow of students so as to satisfy the manpower demands more efficiently – the present application of the manpower approach in the developing countries tends to lead to unsatisfactory results."[9] Let us examine what the major goals of human resource development are, and how complex is their accomplishment.

[7] Frederick Harbison and Charles Myers, *Education, Manpower and Economic Growth* (New York: McGraw-Hill, 1964), p. 235.

[8] A serious limitation of this approach is that it assumes what still needs to be proved. It assumes that because there is now a high correlation between the level of education and national income, the one caused the other.

[9] Richard Bland, "Education and Training in Developing Countries," *International Labour Review*, Vol. 92, No. 6, December 1965, p. 481.

The major objectives of human resource development in under-developed countries could be classified into three broad categories. *First*, a country must develop an educational system which will produce skills needed for various tasks which have to be performed under the developmental scheme(s). *Second*, it must provide useful employment to those who are underemployed or unemployed. Investment in education is of little avail if a country merely concentrates on providing education to its people, without providing the opportunities for them to gainfully apply the acquired skills. After all, skills unutilized are no better than skills not created. *Third*, the plan for educational development must also assist in the evolution of those institutions and personal values which shape attitudes toward productive activity and acceptance of change. If this objective seems the least tangible, it is also perhaps the most important for a developing country.

To state these objectives is to open up Pandora's box of conceptual difficulties and complex questions. For example, what is the distinction between educational expenditures that represent merely consumption and those which represent investment? Is it apt to apply the traditional cost-benefit criterion to expenditure on education or should education be regarded as an end in itself? How does one estimate the costs of and return from investment in human capital?

Another set of questions pertains to the actual planning phase of the educational programs. For example, what should be the time paths of educational expansion in a country? To what extent does education have priority over other goals? For what part of the labor force is literacy essential? What is the minimum level of literacy needed to embark upon a process of modernization? What should be the proportion of technical versus liberal education in the final plans?

As noted earlier, creation of proper skills via educational programs is only part of the task; the other and more important part deals with their effective utilization, related to such questions as: are there circumstances which preclude people from using their skills? Are their barriers to entry into jobs in which their skills would be suitable?

In sum, are the educational schemes attuned to the needs of developmental tasks or are they wasteful and consequently an impediment to economic development? Among these complexities, the one question which poses serious problems both to the planner and the policy maker is that of returns from investment in human capital.

Investment and Returns: Imponderables

There are several factors other than those of a long term nature, which make estimates of return from investment on education for human resource development imponderable. Economists have attempted to solve this problem in various ways. For example, Schultz and others have estimated that in the United States "expenditures on education have increased over 100 times from 1900 to 1956."[10] Denison and Correa[11] have attempted, in fact, to determine what shares of the increase in gross national product in the U.S. can be ascribed to the usual types of capital formation, arguing that the large increase left unaccounted for in this way might legitimately be attributed to improvement in human resources. These attempts manifest the complexity of the problem of estimating returns from investment on human resources. The problem of estimation is compounded in underdeveloped countries by a lack of reliable statistical data.

The development of human resources is a time consuming process, and to state the obvious, investment in this area is a long term investment from an economic point of view. The gains manifest themselves after a relatively long period of gestation. Although education is an item of critical importance it alone cannot assure steady economic progress. And yet, as Harbison and Myers put it, "if a country is unable to develop its human resources, it cannot develop much else."[12] It is this type of interrelationship that pinpoints the importance of investment in this area. Moreover as David McClelland has recently posited, "It should take more than a highly educated populace to produce rapid economic growth. The people have got to want to achieve,

[19] T. W. Schultz, "Investment in Human Capital," *American Economic Review*, LI (March, 1961), pp. 1-17; and "Reflections on Investment in Man," *Journal of Political Economy*, LXX, No. 5 (October, 1962, supplement), pp. 1-8. See also S. J. Mushkin (ed.), *Economics of Higher Education* (Washington: GPO, 1962).

[11] E. F. Denison, *The Residual Factor in Economic Growth* (Paris: OECD, 1963). H. Correa, *The Economics of Human Resources* (Den Haag, Drukkerij Pasmans, 1962).

[12] F. Harbison and C. Myers (*Education, Manpower and Economic Growth.*) *op. cit.*, p. 13.

to care about putting their knowledge to productive uses."[13] What principles should then guide investment in human resources which will produce not only skilled people but people with proper motivation? No attempt is made to answer this question here.

Extent of progress in India's education

India inherited the system of education which in many ways fell short of the national needs. Before independence, 1947, education was a neglected field in the sense little attention was paid to the kind and extent of education which would produce the needed skills and talents. Whatever effort was expended in education it was toward producing a corps of clerical workers who could fill the routine jobs in various governmental departments. India's 700,000 villages escaped even these dubious attributes of the educational system.

The slow progress in education is evidenced by the fact that literacy in 1941 was 14.6 per cent and ten years later, in 1951, it was 18.3 per cent. The stress which a country places on education may be measured in a variety of ways – by literacy rates, by expenditures on education, or by enrollment figures at various levels of instruction. One could take a look at some of the quantitative data available in these areas keeping in mind one important question; namely, has education in India, after 15 years of planned development, emerged as a powerful engine for social and economic progress?

The number of literates per 1000 persons of *all* age groups in 1961 was 339 among males and 128 among females – the average for the group being 237, or approximately 24 per cent. Although no reliable figures reflecting the current situation are available, it would be a reasonable guess to place this figure at less than 30 per cent.

Expenditure on education constitutes one of the largest single non-defense current public expenditures in India. During the First Five-Year Plan education claimed 50 per cent of funds allocated to "Social Services" category. Expenditure on education in 1958-59 was estimated at Rs. 5.5 per capita (or 1.7 per

[13] David McClelland, "Does Education Accelerate Economic Growth?" *Economic Development and Cultural Change*, XIV, No. 3 (April 1966), p. 269.

cent of the national income). In U.S. dollars (before the 1966 devaluation) the per capita expenditure on education in India, in 1961, was remarkably low compared with similar expenditures in Canada ($ 56), United States ($ 92), and the Soviet Union ($ 98). Again, as a proportion of GNP, India's 1.7 per cent spending on education does not favorably compare with Canada's 4.5, U.S.'s 4.6, and Soviet Union's 7.1 per cent. However, currently it stands at about 3 per cent, a definite improvement over the 1961 figure. Mere expansion of this educational input cannot alleviate the problems of education in India because in India's case the problem appears to be one of coordination and reorganization of educational effort rather than the need for physical expansion.

The outlay for general education has indeed successively increased from one plan period to another. It amounted to Rs. 1.33 billion in the First Plan, increased to Rs. 2.08 billion in the Second Plan, to Rs. 4.18 in the Third Plan in which an additional Rs. 1.42 billion were earmarked for technical education. The share of technical education in the total outlay on education has been 13, 19 and 25 per cent in the First, Second, and the Third Plans but curiously 20 per cent in the Fourth Plan which shows a total outlay for all types of education in the amount of about Rs. 12.5 billion.

In contrast to the estimated literacy rates, and outlay on education, the enrollment figures, particularly post-primary school enrollment, are more reliable and more useful.

When India became free there were 173,000 primary schools with an enrollment of 14.11 million children; 18,140 secondary with about 3.4 million students. The total expenditure then was about Rs. 576 million which averaged to Rs. 1.94 per capita. During the first 14 years of independence, there was an almost 100 per cent increase in the number of educational institutions and 163 per cent increase in enrollment. Currently there are 350,000 primary schools with an enrollment of over 52 million children, 70,000 secondary schools with students numbering almost 12 million. The secondary school enrollment shows a fourfold increase since independence.

The post-independence era has been marked by significant gains in the field of technical education. Expenditure which amounted to Rs. 1.42 billion in the Third Plan was far greater than

Rs. 490 million and Rs. 202 million spent on technical education during the Second and the First Plans respectively. The enrollment in 1965-66 was of the order of 23,000 in the degree, and 43,00 in the diploma (certificate) programs. The number of technical institutions has also considerably increased. In 1947 there were 38 degree and 53 certificate awarding institutions but as of 1964-65 there were 131 degree and 200 diploma awarding institutions. There is no doubt that India has taken several steps, since Independence, to expand and strengthen the facilities for technical education to keep pace with the industrialization programs and needs.

The facilities for science education enrollment at the university level increased from 37,030 in 1950-1951 to more than 100,000 to date. The recently initiated Summer Science Institutes have led to the popularization of science.

Under the Fourth Plan the total outlay on education will be twice the amount under the Third Plan and will constitute 8.7 per cent of the total public sector outlay as against 7 per cent in the Third Plan. Thus one could surmise that there will be greater expansion of education in the years to come in India.

Evaluation from the Human Resource Development Viewpoint

Although education must provide the basis for any purposeful development and is obviously necessary for any economic and social progress, indiscriminate expansion of education at all levels and in all directions is neither discreet nor desirable. The recent report of the Education Commission (1966) has called for a "drastic reconstruction," almost a revolution, of the present education system making it "science-based and in coherence with the Indian culture and values" so that it serves as "an instrument for the nation's progress, security, and welfare." The commission has taken a panoramic view of the entire educational system and has recommended changes that touch upon all of its aspects. Even if all the changes as suggested by the Commission are accepted in their entirety, it is clear that their implementation will be a time-consuming process. In the mean time, "India must tackle the educational challenge on two major fronts: the expansion of education to the largest extent possible along with a reconstruction and reshaping of education to suit the needs of a modern, growing, and increasingly complex economy."[14]

In the area of literacy India's performance has been exceedingly poor. Literacy is used by some economists as a criterion for measuring social and economic development.[15] Even otherwise it is a powerful vehicle for transmitting information, for forging integration, and for preparing masses of people to discharge the responsibilities of citizenship in a democracy. It is in the light of this that one notes with some dismay that the rate of literacy even after 19 years of political freedom and planned economic development remains not much above 30 per cent.

If universal primary education is a worthwhile goal, India's progress in achieving this has been spectacular. At the completion of the Third Plan 75 per cent of the nation's children in the age group 6-11 were in schools. The Fourth Plan may witness this proportion to be more than 90 per cent. Spectacular though this progress has been, it has not been devoid of difficulties.[16] One wonders if universal primary education is a goal of such high desirability and should be pursued with such unremitting zeal. Nevertheless, it is much more important for India to improve the quality of primary education than to plan for further expansion merely in quantitative terms.

At the secondary level of education, while progress has been less than satisfactory in quantitative terms, peculiar difficulties have been experienced. Attempts to transform high schools into higher secondary or multipurpose schools and to introduce vocational courses in the curricula have not been very successful. According to a recent study, "secondary education remains a quality bottleneck in India's program of human resource development."[17]

[14] For a general discussion of educational problems in India, see K. G. Saiyidain, *Problems of Educational Reconstruction* (New York: Asia Publish House, 1962).

[15] For example, G. L. Bach, *Economics* (Englewood Cliffs, N.J.: Prentice-Hall, Inc., 1966), p. 283; Don Adams, "Pitfalls and Priorities in Education," in *Dynamics of Development* (New York: Frederick Praeger, 1964), p. 243.

[16] In 1960-61, while 80 per cent of the boys were in school, only 40 per cent of the girls were in school. Many who start school simply do not remain in school long enough to acquire the rudiments of literacy. A recent study reported in *New York Times* (March 20, 1966, p. 16) suggested that only 35% who start first grade complete the fifth grade five years later. There is also a lack of properly trained teachers, inspiring curricula, and sufficient appreciation of the value of education especially in rural parts.

[17] Harbison and Myers, (*Education, Manpower and Economic Growth*) *op. cit.*, p. 113.

A strong and efficient program of secondary education is perhaps the most important ingredient in a plan for human resource development. It must adequately prepare young persons for jobs in industry and business as well as provide a foundation for further education for those pursuing higher education.

Higher education has not undergone much change, although there has been a mushrooming of liberal arts and commerce colleges equipped with less than adequate physical and faculty resources. As a whole there is also an imbalance in the number of students enrolled in liberal arts versus engineering-technical studies. For example, about a million students are studying history, literature, philosophy, economics, and other allied subjects whereas only a third of these are pursuing technical and engineering subjects.

Conclusion

What can be done, and what should be done in the area of human resource development for economic growth in India? The answer could be twofold: one, there are possibilities in so far as educational *policies* are concerned, and two, there are possibilities in so far as *research approaches* are concerned.

Secondary education needs to be diversified and improved at the earliest time possible. The educational authorities should take steps to sever the unhealthy relationship between college degrees and jobs, which is illusory in many cases. The paramount need in the area of higher education is for quality, and for relating higher education more and more to the stages and needs of economic development. Progress in technical education and training has been rapid but care must be exercised in minimizing the waste of resources. In addition to formal technical education, India needs to expand programs of in-plant and on-the-job training. A model is available in the Tata Industries program.

India also faces a greater challenge in the area of teacher training at all levels. So is the challenge of motivation of the teachers. There is a great need to seriously consider the salary structure of teachers at all levels.

There is a considerable "brain-drain" from India. So far as the Indian educated and foreign educated persons now residing abroad are concerned, their returning to India is as much a problem of administration and communication as it is one of finding jobs which they consider suitable. In addition to oral urges, concrete incentive schemes to make India attractive for these people should be put into effect.

If one were to determine, though approximately, the expected returns from investments in human resources, one has to undertake the data-gathering type of research. Post-primary education is likely to be the more important input for economic growth; therefore, it is desirable to gather data and break down these figures into second and third level enrollment ratio because the latter appear to be important for recent economic advances in highly developed countries. Next it is also necessary to distinguish between educations *stocks* and *flows*, for educational stocks must be corrected for the base just as the economic outputs must be.

In sum, quality must be the chief criterion when India contemplates either initiation or expansion of its educational facilities. Education must provide for the transmission of skills and talents which enhance the dignity of work and of the individual even as it forges common bonds among different parts of the country. It has been suggested by some that at the present stage of India's development, returns from physical capital formation are greater than from investment in human capital. Be that as it may, there is an urgent need to recognize the real significance of education and human resource development for economic growth.

CHAPTER 12

CONCLUSION: GENERAL ISSUES

In Western industrial civilization in its formative stages, the entrepreneurs were people who made the key innovations. One thinks of such famous names as Arkwright, Boulton and Bessemer in England; Strousbarg, Thyssen and Krupp in Germany; and Gould, Harriman, Carnegie and Ford in the United States, to cite a few. Besides these clearly exceptional personalities there were men who made minor but still important innovations. Many more were imitators and followers but those imitations involved a considerable degree of initiative and vigor. In sharp contrast, although there has been, for a long time, a number of great entrepreneurial famililies in India (e.g., the Birlas and Tatas) they have had few followers. It seems a characteristic of successful business men in India that they do not stay in a single industry; they start in one and then proceed on to some entirely unrelated industry. In this way the same group may initiate and develop a number of industries, but they do not seem to inspire imitators.

It is clear that in underdeveloped countries such as India the supply of entrepreneurs is limited, in the first place, by economic circumstances, and secondly, by the social structure. Literature on entrepreneurs in different countries abounds, and some of the questions of significant import for inquiry have been: How are we to explain men of the entrepreneurial type? What conditions favored their appearance in large numbers in Western Europe and the United States in the nineteenth century? And what determines their pattern of behavior once they have become entrepreneurs?

Alfred Marshall argued that the most valuable of all capital is that invested in human beings. A growing number of contemporary economists subscribes to a theory – of which Theodore W. Schultz is a leading exponent – that human resources are a form of capital, a produced means of production, and the product of investment. In the final analysis, the relative wealth of a country rests on its power to develop and to effectively utilize the capacities and potentialities of its people.

In his preface to *Educating Tomorrow's Managers* (CED), Theodore Yntema stated that "...the quality of college training for business careers affects not only the probable performance of the economy in the hands of the oncoming generation, but the overall quality of higher education, and indeed, the very health of our society." Yntema's frame of reference was the United States and he was specifically referring to the business majors in the colleges and schools of business in the U.S. The CED report, as well as other studies, was primarily concerned with a fundamental question: Are the collegiate schools of business making the needed contribution to the development of business management so vital to the economic performance of the U.S.

As far as we can tell, the earliest research effort expended in the direction of finding and determining what value the psychological knowledge of human motivation might have in understanding so complex a phenomenon as economic development, is that of David C. McClelland. Some theorists, of course, came to the conclusion, rightly we think, that what is called economic development or economic growth is really more socio-psychological than economic. Economists like W. W. Rostow, for example, have insisted that economic theory must be linked ultimately to sociological and psychological constructs if it is to be maximally useful. As a first step in this direction, he lists several basic "human motives" or "human propensities" which economic analysis suggests are important for development as follows: to develop fundamental science, to apply science to economic ends, to accept innovations, and to seek material advance.

The economists and planners interested in economic growth are engaged in projecting economic growth (in India) on the necessary basis of a crude macro-economic theory of growth which makes many implicit assumptions concerning the operation of the economic system. As Mary CushingNiles, a keen student of India, pointed out quite some time ago "All over the world, people's desires are directed toward higher living standards. These standards can only be raised by: more production through greater productivity per man-hour, less unemployment, more hours worked, or a combination of two or more of these.

In this volume we set out to give expression to the role and importance of what we broadly referred to as "managerialism" in the economic development process, with particular reference to the industrialization aspects. We made the assumption, based upon the experiences of India and other developing countries, that industrial enterprises, especially in the public sector, are beset by various management and organizational problems. We recognize that the experiences of successful enterprises, which constitute at least part of the "theories" in the Western countries, have some relevance in the economic environment of countries such as India.

One may argue that the "management process" school of thought is inadequate as a framework for studying management. This is perhaps true in the case of some large enterprises in contemporary United States. The behavioral science school, which visualizes organizations in terms of interactions of individuals and groups, takes personal development and satisfaction as its key parameters, and often seeks to remove the structural constraints on this fulfillment, and the management science school, which tends to view the organization as a huge man-machine system susceptible to modification in terms of mathematical models, both have contributions to make even in the Indian economic environment.

The management process school, despite its limitations, seems to us to be the most fruitful frame of reference for the study of management phenomenon in the Indian context. The reasons why we think so are: (a) Management in India is a relatively new phenomenon; it is not comparable to management as it prevails now in the United States (perhaps it is more comparable to management of enterprises in the United States as of the early 1900's). (2) The so-called principles of management which exemplify the "management process school" are a double edged sword. If they are employed with skill and with discretion, they can be useful in defining and refining management. Applied insistently and inflexibly, they can result in a rigid, bureaucratic organization structure poorly attuned to a company's unique needs.

Most of these principles are no more than generalizations about what has been observed to work in practice, based on past enterprise experience. Being derived and distilled from experience in the management of large scale enterprises, they are certainly subject to revision in the light of new experiences as they are happening in the United States, or in the light of new circumstances as they have arisen in India. One of the strongest criticisms levelled against the so-called principles of management and organization, especially by behavioral scientists, is that they are not empirically based. We have in the volume made various suggestions to test them empirically in India.

With this background information about the nature of our inquiry, let us summarize the conclusions first, and then raise some general issues for further research. The following are the general conclusions:

1. The managers of the industrial enterprises in India lacked the attributes of professionals in the early part of the twentieth century, and until the political independence which came to India in 1947, the dominant style of management was that of "managing agency system."

2. There is a new system of management in India now and this is producing a new kind of manager whose education and training professionally is rising, and who is growingly conscious of his image as a "manager." While it is difficult to characterize the present status of enterprise management in India, it can be said that it is becoming more professionalized than before.

3. While it is becoming professionalized, there is still ample room for systematic study of the phenomenon. This is true of most countries including the United States. Scientific inquiry entails a juxtaposition of theory and empirical evidence. One set of hypotheses which appear to have significance in India or elsewhere relates to enterprise "goal- setting" and "decision-making."

4. While the phenomenon of modern management is essentially an American product, systematic inquiry is likely to reveal the applicability of many American management tools and techniques in the Indian context. In order to pursue this research, a model as suggested, appears to yield the most fruitful results.

5. The organization of public enterprises in India has failed to give adequate recognition to the effective utilization of human resources, and hence to their productivity. The first and foremost thing to remedy this situation is to place first class, full time, professionally trained management men in the top

positions and give them the latitude to work out solutions.

6. Behavioral science research within the organizations do provide managers with useful information which could imaginatively be used for the good of the workers as well as that of the enterprise. (For an example, see the Appendix.)

One of the goals of bringing out this volume was to suggest specific research areas where efforts could be expended in a worthwhile manner. Exploratory through the treatment in these chapters has been, there appear to be several avenues for further empirical research in depth.

The most pressing need for further research is in the area of organization and management of the existing large public sector industrial enterprises. These institutions are already there although performing below par. While it is not difficult to suggest the economic contributions which these institutions should make to the overall development in a country, it is difficult to trace the significant variables that are impeding these institutions from making those contributions. The only research that can make any headway is "pooled research." By this we mean that it should involve not only researchers but also others including the enterprise managers, the governmental administrators, legislators, and the workers.

Specifically we suggest the following issues as essential to enhance managerialism in India. They are:

1. To find out if the Western-type management does enhance the efficiency and effectiveness of the large-scale enterprises, an experiment entailing the introduction of adaptable elements of Western management know-how within the public sector, should be undertaken. Both the "control" and the "experimental" organizations could be part of the public sector.

2. To set the "goal" for the public sector enterprises, an experimental study entailing a single motive public enterprise and a multimotive public enterprise can be made. The single motive may be defined as the profit motive: multimotive as profit and specific social motives.

3. To find out the peculiar difficulties of public ownership and management, comparative studies with respect to internal management between comparable public sector and private sector firms in given industries can be made.

4. To assess the value of management education as it is now imparted in educational institutions in India, an evaluation *not* by foreign experts but by the country's own nationals who are working abroad either in industry or educational institutions should be made.

In fine, what we have said in this volume is neither complete nor conclusive. We have not said that enhancement of managerialism alone will produce economic miracles and wipe out poverty and squalor in India. Our approach has been to confine ourselves to one aspect of the magnanimous question of economic development, and being academicians have pointed out some of the workable theories, workable frames of reference, and approaches. It is, of course, up to the policy-makers to promote such research and find out if these hypotheses yield fruitful results for improving the management situation. Our strong belief is that they will, and that there certainly is room for managerial experimentation as a part of the large-scale socio-economic experimentations which countries like India and others are now conducting. An initiative taken by one underdeveloped country may have something to offer to other nations which are also in similar predicaments.

One last point. We do recognize that the current food crisis in India accompanied by an ever increasing population (12 million per annum) have forced the policy makers to examine more seriously than before agricultural and farm production. While we foresee further attempts to augment to resolve the food crisis, we do not expect "denationalization" of industry in the public sector. But there is a chance that economic planning may be de-emphasized. That is all the more of a cogent reason to delve deeply into the problems of existing industries, both in the public and private sector, with a view to making them productive in the fullest sense of the word.

APPICATION OF INDUSTRIAL PSYCHOLOGY*

Industrial psychology, which in recent years has more generally been referred to as occupational psychology, is concerned with the behavior of people
at work. As with any other science it started as a purely descriptive study, with
the observation and recording of what took place. The organizing and classi-
fying of such observation has continued for half a century, and at the same time
general theories have been put forward and experimental studies have been
conducted over a wide area of human behavior.

The very title "industrial psychology" indicates that the science had its
beginnings in industrial societies. In Great Britain the first time that industrial
psychology appeared to have importance at the national level was when, under
the pressure of war in 1916, psychologists were employed to apply their skills
in the struggle for higher industrial output in the munitions industry. Since
then it has been in the most highly industrial countries – particularly the United
States – and at times when the demand for industrial and technological efficiency has been greatest – for example in wartime and in missle and space
exploration development – that the need for industrial psychology has been
most apparent, and the demand for more and more psychological research has
been strongest.

Historically, there is some evidence that the demands for industrial psychology are related to the degree of industrialization and technological development
of a country. Putting this another way, it could be said that as industry grows
and develops so does the need for industrial psychology become more apparent
and more actively felt.

A common conclusion from these facts is that industrial psychology is of
greatest importance and has maximum application in highly industrialized
countries, and that conversely it has little application and is of little importance
to the developing countries. Such an argument is, however, neither logical nor
valid. It would be the equivalent of saying that there is greater need for vitamin
tablets in the United States, where a substantial proportion of the population
feel they should – and do – consume them, than in Africa or South-East Asia,
where relatively few people have heard of vitamins and there is thus no widespread demand. We have to distinguish between real and actual needs as as-
sessed by an objective observer, and felt needs as experienced by people themselves. It is true that industrialized countries are now recognizing that they
can ignore the knowledge vested in industrial psychology only at their peril;
but does it follow that the basic principles and the application of industrial
psychology has little to offer the developing countries? The experience of the

* Reprinted with permission from the *International Labour Review*, Vol. 92, No. 4,
October 1965. Original title of the article was "The Application of Industrial Psy-
chology to Developing Countries." The author, H. G. Maule, is a Senior Lecturer in
Occupational Psychology at the London School of Hygiene and Tropical Medicine.

Psychology Division of the Central Labour Institute of the Ministry of Labour and Employment, India, and of other organizations in India suggests that there at any rate psychology has an important part to play in the development of industry. But before examining the proposition it is necessary to give a brief account of the nature and scope of industrial psychology.

The nature and scope of industrial psychology

In its broadest sense industrial psychology, though concerned with the behavior of people at work, could include all the home and social pressures outside the factory that have their repercussions on working behavior. A line has to be drawn somewhere and as a rule the industrial psychologist fixes his attention more on working environment than on the numerous experiences and attitudes that belong more to a worker's leisure hours and home conditions.

There is no hard and fast classification of industrial psychology. The tendency in the United Kingdom is to consider the whole field under two main headings, namely (a) fitting the man to the job, which includes selection, training, and so on, and (b) fitting the job to the man, including the arrangement and organization of work and the interaction between operator and working environment.

The items that would be contained in such a classification do not differ substantially from those included in the article published in the International Labour Review in 1960 under the title "Current trends in industrial psychology." Industrial psychology is defined there as "the scientific study of human behavior and experience within the context of work," but the article goes on to state that since psychology itself is still not a unified, integrated science it is not surprising that the field of industrial psychology is still evolving and not precisely defined...

Some theoretical considerations on the applicability of industrial psychology to India

In contemporary Indian industry the whole range of industrial plant and equipment is to be found – from the simple village industries of hand spinning and weaving to highly automated factory industries such as electrical generation, chemical industries, engineering, aircraft and so on.

Experience from Western countries shows only too often that the time to prevent the error of design and to inculcate an awareness of the significance and meaning of ergonomics or human engineering is not *after* mistakes have been made, but before, so that they can be avoided. Even with hand tools and with simple machinery the problem of their appropriateness to the human operator needs to be studied. In the most highly developed Indian industries the need is quite clearly similar to that of the highly industrialized countries.

In the West it has been shown over a period of more than half a century that neither the best length of working day or working week nor the best arrangement of work and rest within the working day are always in operation. From the mid-nineteenth century to the present time there have been abundant examples of inappropriate working hours, sometimes despite available knowledge and sometimes in times of acute national need. It is hard (indeed it is impossible) to believe that India too is not making some of the same mistakes.

Studies by Indian psychologists of the performance of night-shift workers in a chemical works have revealed that as much as 20 per cent of the working time may be spent away from work. Whatever the reasons for this, the result is that the best use is not made of the available machinery and equipment. In India there is an abundance of manpower but too little machinery. It is therefore of the greatest importance to ensure optimum machine utilization; and this is closely related to the effective use of manpower. As long ago as 1895 Sir William Mather said, speaking of daily hours of work: "Of this I am assured, that the most economical production is obtained by employing men only so long as they are at their best – when this is passed there is no true economy in their continued work." This was true in 1895 and it is still true today.

There are abundant other examples to suggest that neither are the most suitable people always found for particular occupations, as indicated in the preceding section, nor are the best conditions created in which the worker can operate most effectively.

The following section discusses some Indian research studies, in the field of attitudes, morale and motivation, carried out by Indian psychologists with expert aid from the International Labour Office.

Some practical experiences in India

During the past three years an I.L.O. sponsored team has undertaken a series of studies in India to measure attitudes and morale of workers and of junior and middle management, and to relate these rather intangible things to industrial efficiency.

A chemical process undertaking

The first of these studies was concerned with the attitudes and morale of managers and workers in three units of a large chemical process undertaking. In each unit managers and workers alike were asked the views and attitudes toward their supervisors, work benefits, working conditions, promotion policy, and unions. In addition management was asked about salary, personnel progress and communications, as well as various other matters.

The techniques used in interviewing were similar to well-established techniques that have been developed and used in America and Europe. It might well have been argued that these techniques are rather sophisticated for a country only in its early stages of industrial democracy. Nevertheless a rather short interview of a non-directive type was found to be suitable and effective. It was suitable in that practically without exception all the selected personnel were willing to be interviewed, and effective in that it evidently revealed information which was valid and significant.

In the three units of the organization the attitudes and morale were, on some issues, widely divergent. For example, in the oldest unit on almost every point there was an excess of unfavorable over favorable attitudes. Apart from the personal relationships between individuals there was a monotonous and excessive volume of unfavorable responses. On certain items (e.g., selection and promotion practices) there was scarcely a good word said. The over-all conclusions in this unit were unavoidable; there was urgent need for completely restructuring the organization at management level. There were few organizational errors that had not been made and few of the basic requirements that had been adopted. In this instance it was possible to make far-reaching recommendations about communications, policy for benefits and promotion, the practice of delegating authority and the general welfare arrangements.

If the survey had not been undertaken it is very doubtful whether top management would have recognized the precarious position into which the organization had fallen. The recommendations included substantial rethinking about the relations between the unit and its head office, which was located a long way off and appeared to be at the same time excessively authoritarian and inaccessible.

Although the other two units (which were in different parts of India) were found to have a more satisfactory morale than the first, there were a number of areas in which a laissez-faire policy seemed to be leading to a sharp decline in morale and well-being with a consequent threat to performance. There were symptoms of potential trouble, but if prompt remedial action were taken there were good reasons for believing that such trouble could be avoided.

There can be little doubt that this survey demonstrated to the top management that they could very easily be seriously wrong in their assumption about the adequacy of the organization. Although middle management and the workers recognized that all was not well, they had not the facilities nor the ability to pinpoint those things most in need of reexamination and overhaul. And there is little doubt that but for the investigations things would have been left to drift. The significant contribution of the outside, professional scientific investigator is that he can bring his findings directly to the notice of those in whose hands lies the power to take remedial action, whereas without this contribution top management may remain inactive and in ignorance.

By the time I.L.O. assistance came to an end, management was taking some specific action along the lines recommended. Serious consideration had been given to the practicability of a follow-up to investigate the effects of such changes, but this was considered premature. There is every reason to suppose that the Indian psychologists who are continuing the work of the original investigators will, in due time, be in a position to follow up the actions taken as a result of this inquiry.

A cotton textile factory

Two other studies were carried out in 1964 in a large cotton textile factory employing some 10,000 workers. It is the task of the junior and middle management officers in this, as in any company, to form the link between top management, with its policy-forming responsibilities, and the workers, whose job it is to turn raw material – cotton – into the finished product – cotton cloth.

The extent to which officers can succeed in this depends in part upon their attitudes toward company policy and toward their own superiors through whom instructions are given from above. In part it depends upon their attitudes toward their own jobs, and their wish or willingness to do them to the best of their ability.

The task facing the investigators was at two levels. On the one hand it was a straightforward attempt to measure attitudes and feelings and to relate them to other criteria. Secondly, and perhaps more importantly, it was to test whether the techniques that have been well established in Western countries could usefully be employed in India.

The studies that are described took place in two units of the organization. The firm itself had a history of generally progressive management. Many advanced ideas had been initiated in this company. One of the two units was the oldest in the organization and the other, one of the most recent. Not only was the older Mill located in older buildings but it was hardly affected by the rapidly changing managerial practices which were taking place in the newer mill. The two were therefore representative on the one hand of a relatively good but rather conventional outlook and, on the other, of a very progressive approach to the role and function of management.

In the older unit a random sample of three out of four of the officers was interviewed in private – a – confidential interview in which both "open" and "closed" questions were used. During the interview, which lasted about $1\frac{1}{2}$

hours, a good deal of background information was obtained on each officer's experience and training whether with the present company or with another employer. From this part of the inquiry certain patterns emerged.

The average senior officer in charge of a department was 52 years of age and had 24 years' service in the company. He was unlikely to have worked outside the textile industry but stood a 50 per cent chance of having worked in another textile firm.

Below him was a hierarchy from senior to junior assistants, including a number who would appear to have reached the top of their grade and could not reasonably look for further promotion; these men had often spent from 20 to 30 years with the company, having risen from the lowest ranks of operative to their present positions. The younger men, all those under 30, had full university education; but only a small proportion (20 per cent) of the men over 50 had been to a university. Nearly half of the over-50s had no better academic qualification than matriculation. With the rapid advances in scientific education that are taking place all over the world it is by no means surprising to find that young, recently qualified scientists tend to feel that their older colleagues are out of date. New techniques and new developments, learned by youg men in their ordinary recent training, may be unfamiliar to their seniors, despite the fact that the latter have good practical experience.

In a country like India this tendency is aggravated by the tremendous expansion that has taken place in education in the past 20 years. Opportunities for university and other higher education which are taken for granted by those under 30 were not available when those now over 50 were of student age. Thus the gap between the outlook of the older and the younger personnel is accentuated by the recent rapid development of Indian education and scientific training.

This situation tends to make for friction. The older men may feel keenly their lack of theoretical training and so exaggerate the virtues of experience over training, while the younger men are inclined to be impatient with a situation in which their qualifications appear to be undervalued.

Although in an intuitive way the management was aware that this problem existed, they had no way of knowing the extent to which it was a source of frustration at either the senior or the junior level and had therefore not given any serious thought to ways that might be adopted to meet the difficulties it caused.

The major part of the interviews held was concerned with the attitudes of officers toward certain rather well-defined aspects of their work including their prospects in the company, communications or the flow of information upwards and downwards, and the nature of their own authority, the responsibility vested in themselves and their opportunity to make decisions.

By means of a combination of questions with alternative answers and free response to general questions, a very clear picture was obtained of how each individual saw the particular situation and how he felt about what he saw. There could be little doubt about the general validity of the answers. It also became apparent that there were widely divergent attitudes among the different sections of the management. Some of the most extreme variations that were recorded occurred between different departments and there was abundant evidence of successful leadership in some departments and of the almost total failure of leadership in others.

The results also indicated those areas in which the unit as a whole was generating most dissatisfaction. This was the absence of any adequate or satisfactory channels of communication, either from the "board room" downwards or from the junior manager upwards. In the matter of promotion there were indications that the over-all policy of the firm was too strong for any individual departmental manager greatly to influence it, and that discontent was widespread. Even so, in particular departments factors such as age structure made the position even more unsatisfactory.

One of the features of this study was the recognition by many of those interviewed that the unfavorable climate, the lack of delegation of authority, and the inadequacy of communication between themselves and the upper hierarchy of the company, lead directly and sometimes inevitably to loss of productive potential. Inaction, or deliberate "wrong" action, was attributed to the alleged defects in management practice, particularly its unwillingness to delegate responsibility.

There was a substantial volume of evidence, both in the interviews and from other sources, that the interview program produced a deep sense of satisfaction and relief among the staff. It was described as "the best thing that has ever happened" and "the beginning of a new era" – either of which comments might equally have been reported from a similar survey in a Western country.

The top management showed a very real interest in the final report and immediately examined the concluding recommendations with a view to finding the best way to implement them.

Certain senior members of management were inclined to cast doubt on the validity of some of the general findings, but an explanation of the way in which attitudes had been scaled and quantified seemed to reassure and convince them. After discussion between the research team, top management and the individuals concerned, they seemed to accept the over-all accuracy of the findings.

A progressive textile mill

The last study to be discussed here concerns one of the most modern units of the same textile company as that of the preceding survey. The recent history of this particular unit distinguished it from the others in the organization.

A few years previously a young director had been appointed and he had quickly begun to introduce a new orientation to policy, including some of the management techniques that he himself had learned as a student in the United States.

The main features of this policy were as follows:

(1) Young Indian specialists were appointed, some of them trained overseas with postgraduate training in operational research, industrial engineering, quality control, and similar specialties.

(2) Devices were introduced explicitly for the democratization and delegation of management functions. These devices included the appointment of a number of committees of management at which appropriate representatives of each department had equal opportunity and equal rights to raise and discuss any matter on equal terms with others.

(3) A new personnel department was started, under the charge of qualified personnel officers.

(4) Senior posts were opened to applicants from outside the organization, a departure from the former and usual practice of filling all senior posts from within.

The period of most active innovation was from 1960 to 1963. In 1964 it was thought appropriate to attempt to measure some of the results and to try to assess the attitudes toward the change introduced of all the staff at management level. The Industrial Psychology Division of the Central Labour Institute and an I.L.O. expert planned and carried out this investigation.

In one sense the object of the study was to assess the impact of these managerial changes on the officers in the company so as to help the particular firm evaluate the success of its policies in these terms. But from another point of view the object was of a more general kind. This was to ascertain whether a "managerial revolution" could be carried out in a developing country without undue disruption within the managerial ranks; could a progressive approach to management developed from the experience of highly industrialized Western countries be introduced and accepted in a developing country? Finally it was a test for the method of investigation itself, and would demonstrate the practicability of the Western approach to an Asian situation.

The technique used was that of the personal confidential interview with a prepared questionnaire. All the firm's junior and middle management personnel were interviewed. Basic information was obtained from the whole group about their age, length of service, basic education, employment experience and training; those who had been employed in the firm since before the period of change were asked to make comparisons between conditions before the change and conditions at the time of interview. They were asked whether they considered the changes had had any impact on themselves, and if so whether they were for the better or for the worse.

Everyone, whether he had been employed before the changes were first introduced or not, was asked to express his views on certain of the new features – e.g., the value of the committees of management – and all were asked if they had any general comments to make about present conditions.

It had been a feature of this firm to provide a considerable amount of training in both textile technology and management, and views on these training courses were obtained. It became quite evident that training was highly appreciated, and well over half the respondents named additional training they would like to have.

It also became evident that, except in certain fairly well-defined areas, the changes had evoked much more favorable than unfavorable attitudes. In considering the actual content of their work all but a relatively small minority found that it had become more varied, more difficult and more interesting in the past two or three years. The number who recorded greater interest in their work content was more than half the total number interviewed. About a quarter thought there had been no measurable change in the work interest and a very small minority thought the change had been in the wrong direction – that is, the work had become less interesting.

The area in which the greatest change for the better was recorded was the amount of responsibility that an officer felt he had. Those who felt they were now expected to take more responsibility outnumbered the remainder by nearly two to one. It was quite evident that these officers were well pleased with the change, whereas the few who felt that their responsibility had been reduced were highly dissatisfied.

All of the more senior members felt, too, that they were now more involved in taking part in decision-making than formerly, though a few of the more junior people felt that the trend had been in the opposite direction. Here again it was evident that those who felt more involved in decision-making were satisfied, while those who felt less involved were dissatisfied with the change. There was clear evidence that most of these people wanted to take part in the decisions that affected them.

In the matter of their prospects of promotion and their chances of recognition by the company the most junior officers recorded a change for the worse. The same group made up nearly all of those who felt less well informed about the company plans and less able to pass their views upward to top management.

Generally the changes were much less well received by the more junior people than by their seniors. In these ways the survey was able to pinpoint rather clearly that in some respects the changes in policy had been a partial failure, though on the whole there was a remarkable measure of success. In one sense the details of the findings are not important to the general theme of this article. The important thing is that the techniques used were undoubtedly able to fulfill their stated objective.

In the part of the inquiry that made use of the structured interview with some element of prepared alternative responses, the respondents were able, with a few exceptions, to give honest answers which proved amenable to closer statistical examination and quantification. Equally in the final stages of the interview when "free comments" were invited respondents were willing and able to speak freely and without fear of the consequences. It had, at the outset, been made absolutely clear that there was no possibility that the individuals who made comments would become known to top management. All interviewees had been promised that any report on the survey would be available to themselves as well as to the directors. They had also been promised the opportunity of full and open discussion with the investigators of the findings of the survey. There is not the slightest doubt that these promises were accepted by the majority from the outset, and as they were seen to be fulfilled there were signs of growing confidence...

Summary and Conclusion

It has been suggested that there is a belief that sophisticated social sciences are applicable only in sophisticated societies, and that a science such as industrial psychology may therefore have little application in a country that is not already highly industrialized.

But should we accept this view? It has been argued in this article that only by adopting such modern ideas as, for example, human engineering can a developing country hope to avoid many of the serious errors in the design of machines and equipment which were and still are being made in the highly industrialized countries.

During the period the first Industrial Revolution countries made costly mistakes, and currently during the revolution of automation they are still making them. The developing countries, in the process of change from rural and domestic to urban and factory industry, would be wise to examine the mistakes of the West and learn what they can from them. Evidence has been offered to show that in at least one branch of industrial psychology joint teams of Indian and Western psychologists, working through the auspices of the International Labour Office, have demonstrated the practicability and usefulness of the industrial psychologist's methods.

It is not always easy to assess the success of an attitude survey but in the cases that are described a number of advantages can be claimed.

(1) With the exception of a very small minority of individuals, both managers and workers were willing to cooperate fully with the trained interviewers. They accepted without reserve the confidential nature of the interview and were able to speak quite freely about themselves, their work and their firm.

(2) The feeling of relief that is characteristically reported as an accompa-

niment of an attitude survey in the United Kingdom was equally clearly recorded in the Indian surveys.

(3) The attitudes revealed indicated that the traditional, somewhat authoritarian management had some very severe limitations. The potential ability of employees was not realized and, more damaging than this, specific inefficiency was shown to result.

(4) Schemes that, from an objective assessment, appeared to have merit produced antagonism and suspicion because they were not adequately explained or understood.

(5) One Survey demonstrated that the very considerable changes that had been introduced had, on the whole, been accepted and were approved by many of those whose jobs had been most affected.

(6) Contrary to widespread belief, people who were given additional responsibility as well as the authority necessary to shoulder it were well pleased with their changed role. Those who regarded their responsibility as too restricted for their position and status were greatly dissatisfied with the position.

(7) Top management accepted the validity of the findings of the surveys and examined and discussed the recommendations with a view to implementation.

In conclusion we may report the words of the director of the unit in which one of these surveys was conducted. He said: "Most firms, good or bad, would be advised to make use of the techniques of the social sciences and the skills of trained scientists to improve their knowledge of how employees feel about work. They should use this knowledge to guide their policy and their managerial practice."

Together these points lead to the inescapable conclusion that, at least in some of its branches, industrial psychology has an important and immediate part to play in the industrial progress of a developing country.

INDEX

ranking, 76
Controlling, 72, 73, 76
Correa, 144
Corruption, 50
Cyert, Richard, 47
  and J. March, 56
Dahl and Lindblom, 54
Damodar Valley Corporation, 60
Decision-making, 5, 46, 58, 59, 61, 63, 123
  Process, 47, 59, 61, 63, 64
  theories, 55
  unit, 56
Delhi, 91
"democratic management," 47
Denmark, 140
Dennison, 144
Dill, W. R., 54, 66, 69
Directing, 72, 76
Direction, Leadership and Motivation, 74
Discrimination, 28
"distance, technological," 137
Dusseldorf, 124
Education, 23
  in Management, 6
Education Commission (1966), 147
Education, formal, 24, 25
Effective Management, 99
Effectiveness, concept of, 50
English Electric Company, 121
Entrepreneur, 5, 56, 97, 101
  -manager, 98, 99
  class, 6
  goals, 57, 58
Entrepreneur, innovating small, 97
Farmer, R. and Richman, B., 66, 67
Favoritism, 44
Fayol, Henri, 47
Finland, 141
Five-Year Plan(s), 114, 117
  First, 39, 82, 145
  Third, 31, 82
  Fourth, 49, 114, 131
Follett, Mary P., 47, 53
Ford, 151
  Foundation, 37, 105, 106, 109
Foreign Exchange Regulation, Act of 1947, 122
Foreign
  investments, 6, 16
  private investment, 113

ventures, 114
Fortune magazine, 24
French and Israel, 66
Gardner and Moore, 53
Gaus, 53
Germany, 102
Ghana, 102
Goal, concensual, 56
Goal-setting, 5, 13, 46, 55, 56, 58, 64
Goals, legislators', 57
Gonzalez and McMillan, 66, 67
Gould, 151
Government
  and Community, 76
  of India, 16, 38, 137, 138
Great Britain, 141
Greece, 79
Gross, Bertram M., 50, 51
Gujarat, 31, 32
  and Maharastra, 31
Harbison, Frederick, 142, 144
  and Burgess, 66
  and Myers, 21, 68
Harriman, 151
Hartman, 66
Harvard School of Business Administration, 35, 106, 109
Hawthorne studies, 51
"head-clerk" image, 33
Henley-on-Thames, 34, 36
hierarchy, 52
Hindus, 11, 13, 28, 29, 32
  and Sikh, 29
Hindustan Lever, 105
Hindustan Machine Tools, 85
Hoffman-LaRoche, 121
Human
  capital, 139, 140
  factor, 139
  research, 83, 92
I.L.O. (International Labour Organization), 39
Imperial Chemical Industries, 118
Indian
  Administrative Service, 88
  Airlines Corp., 16
  Civil Service, 68
  Companies Act of 1913, 15
  Companies Act, 1956, 15
  "experiment," 130
  industrialization, 10
  Institute of Management, 35, 39, 109